CAN'T HELP MYSELF

Also by Meredith Goldstein

The Singles

CAN'T HELP MYSELF

Lessons and Confessions from a Modern Advice Columnist

MEREDITH GOLDSTEIN

Author of *The Boston Globe*'s Love Letters column

GRAND CENTRAL PUBLISHING

NEW YORK BOSTON

Grand Central Publishing
Hachette Book Group
1290 Avenue of the Americas
New York, NY 10104
grandcentralpublishing.com
twitter.com/grandcentralpub

First Edition: April 2018

Grand Central Publishing is a division of Hachette Book Group, Inc. The Grand Central Publishing name and logo is a trademark of Hachette Book Group, Inc.

The publisher is not responsible for websites (or their content) that are not owned by the publisher.

Library of Congress Cataloging-in-Publication Data has been applied for.

ISBN 978-1-4555-4377-9 (hardcover)
ISBN 978-1-4555-4378-6 (ebook)

Printed in the United States of America

LSC-H

10 9 8 7 6 5 4 3 2 1

For my sister, Brette Goldstein, the most interesting character.

Contents

Introduction

This is a memoir told in stories and letters. It's what happened, as I remember it, and my sister says my memory is pretty good.

Some names and details have been conflated and changed, mostly to protect innocent people who took me to the Cheesecake Factory.

—Meredith

CAN'T HELP MYSELF

Chapter 1

Help Me, Help You

It was not a good time to start writing an advice column.

I was not at my best. Not in 2008.

I'd always been good at helping friends with their problems; I was the consoling, honest confidante who could make anyone feel better about a breakup or a bad first date.

But during that long period of dejection, which lasted a full twelve months, I was the woman crying near the vending machines at work.

I had a special spot where I liked to turn into a puddle—next to two snack machines in the old *Boston Globe* pressroom where they prepared the circulars, those colorful ads with coupons that fit inside your newspaper.

I'd sink to the floor, under the glow of the Coke logo, and weep, usually for about seven to eight minutes at a time. Sometimes no tears would come, and I'd dry-heave like the wind had been knocked out of me. Sometimes it was a Claire Danes *Homeland* cry, with a trembling chin and angry whimpers.

The vending machines were just out of the way of the spot where broad-shouldered men with Boston accents brought stacks of newspapers to and from a freight elevator. If those guys noticed me in tears, they didn't let on.

I'm sure they did notice, though, because my nose blows were mighty, like the trumpet of an elephant, thanks to my sinus polyps, which, according to my ear, nose, and throat doctor, are "very impressive."

I'd never been a big crier, but back then, I couldn't stop myself from weeping about Patrick, my ex-boyfriend and coworker, who'd dumped me when I'd least expected it. Patrick, who took me to dinner by the beach and bought me cotton candy at Fenway Park. Patrick, who was the tallest guy I'd ever dated (6'6"!). Patrick, whose emails about our colleagues were so deliciously sarcastic that often I'd have to minimize them seconds after I received them so that no one near my cubicle would see.

Sometimes I'd cry about Patrick because I'd accidentally crossed paths with him in the *Globe* cafeteria. That kind of run-in was devastating, because he always looked content and relaxed—like the breakup hadn't ruined his life. He wore his everyday khakis and button-down suit shirt, and chatted with coworkers with an easy smile on his face. I'd hide behind the cafeteria plants thinking, "How dare he. How dare he eat."

Other times I cried because I *hadn't* run into Patrick.

Early on, I thought it would feel better to avoid him, so for the first few months after the breakup I brought a toaster to the office to make my English muffins at my desk. No more cafeteria for me. I would live in my cubicle like it was a panic room.

But all the toaster did was attract mice—there were shit pellets everywhere—and I was no less miserable. Avoiding Patrick made me feel like he could just disappear, like our closeness had never happened.

I just wanted him back. I wanted him to run to my desk and tell me he'd made a mistake by letting me go.

"I miss you," he would say in my fantasies, with the slight Boston accent that got worse when he was drinking. "Let's go get burgers."

I was miserable without Patrick—but I never wanted to marry him. I didn't want to have babies with him. I never even thought we'd move in together.

The truth was that the breakup devastated me because I had *no intention* of marrying Patrick. I'd decided—during our short relationship—that he might be an alternative to everything I didn't want.

As I entered my thirties, I was surrounded by peers who were either married or looking to be, but I didn't see myself on that path. I couldn't imagine living with anyone besides friends, and I had no desire to have kids.

Maybe it had something to do with my mom, who gave up a piano performance career to marry my dad, only to get a divorce. She always said she loved raising my sister and me, and that on most days, teaching piano lessons in our living room was a more rewarding use of her Juilliard degrees, but I couldn't imagine making those sacrifices for a relationship. I *liked* putting work first, and I loved my freedom.

But that didn't mean I wanted to be alone.

Patrick, a Massachusetts-bred sports fan who worked in the paper's advertising department, was thirty-seven when we met and seemed to share my lack of interest in marriage and kids. He'd managed to avoid marrying two decades' worth of girlfriends, and still lived in a Brookline condo he'd bought after graduating from Holy Cross. He enjoyed his status quo, just like me.

It all started when he approached me in the cafeteria to tell me he liked my writing, specifically my stories about nightlife and things to do around the city.

"I'm Patrick, from the advertising department," he said with a big smile. "I liked your story the other day."

He was blond with broad shoulders and looked like the kind of guy who had masculine nicknames in high school. Like Champ. Or Kicker.

After a few more inevitable run-ins around the building, we started to email. Then we traded phone numbers and began texting. Months later, we shared our first meal outside of work.

It took us even more months to admit that our regular dinners, most of which were at the Cheesecake Factory, were probably dates. I began sleeping over, sometimes wearing his oversized Timberwolves T-shirt.

I'd never dated the kind of guy who had a Timberwolves T-shirt. I didn't care enough to ask why he was a fan of a team in Minnesota—I didn't even know what sport the Timberwolves played—but I was happy to wear the uniform.

I fell hard for Patrick and adored all of the ways he was one hundred percent himself—and my opposite. He refused to try new foods, loved the Pogues, and liked to vacation in places like Las Vegas. When bad things happened, he'd spit out one of his many catchphrases: "Sucks to suck."

People at work were shocked to find out we were dating.

Patrick, who was beloved at the *Globe*, was Catholic, stoic, and kept a stack of baseball biographies on his nightstand, whereas I was a Jewish over-sharer who slept near a copy of *Harry Potter*. It didn't matter, though; on nights we were both free, we could be happy together, ordering fast food, my feet in his lap as we watched television.

The thing I liked most about our relationship was that it was always about respecting each other's separate routines as opposed to combining them. I'd text him while he was out at bars with friends, but never expected to come along. I never felt bad going to a party without Patrick because he never worried about missing out. We could always get together after and talk about the highlights.

While other couples I knew took big next steps, Patrick and I stood still. I started to believe that we could maintain our noncommittal cable watching for the rest of our lives—that perhaps two people who weren't fond of change were meant to stay exactly the same, together.

When he broke up with me, a move I hadn't seen coming, he sat me down on his beige Jordan's Furniture couch, under his framed 2004 Boston Red Sox World Series championship mementos, and said something like, "I just don't see this going anywhere," and I thought, "Me neither!"

I didn't want to go anywhere with Patrick. That was the point.

But it turned out Patrick was looking for a lot more. He was interested in new experiences and considered his lifestyle to be temporary. He wanted a real partner—maybe a wife—and I wasn't even close to what he imagined for himself. He just hadn't said so.

I didn't know where that left me, but I feared the answer was: alone.

After it was over, something changed in me. I stayed home a lot because I didn't want to hang out with couples. I also avoided single people because they depressed me. I became a mediocre friend.

At night, I re-watched every season of *Buffy the Vampire Slayer*, because Buffy had been through worse, and it made me feel like I had a destiny. Sometimes I'd watch the same episode a few times in a row while eating frozen waffles in bed.

If I ran into Patrick at work, face-to-face, my instinct was to bolt before he could talk to me. On rare occasions, though, I'd confront him, looking for more answers.

One time I spotted him in the parking lot, near the rows of green *Globe* delivery trucks, and approached him, telling him that he'd "ruined the Cheesecake Factory for me."

That is something I said out loud.

"I can't even go there anymore," I told him. "The Cheesecake Factory was *our thing*, and now I can't even set foot inside without getting upset."

"Nope," Patrick said, not letting that one pass. "I'm going to have to stop you right there. I did *not* ruin the fucking Cheesecake Factory for you, and you know it. You go to the Cheesecake Factory with *everyone you know*. You were going to the Cheesecake Factory long before I was around."

He was right. I went to the Cheesecake Factory with everyone.

"But now the Cheesecake Factory makes me think of *you*," I whined, and then grimaced, because I was embarrassed by the person I'd become.

I was self-aware enough to know that with my blubbering and begging, I was one pint of ice cream and a flannel blanket away from becoming a more sedentary Bridget Jones, but I couldn't stop myself. Sometimes breakups turn you into the kind of person you wouldn't befriend in a million years. Sometimes they turn you into a caricature.

In other words, sucks to suck.

It was shortly after the Cheesecake Factory meltdown that my *Boston Globe* editors considered an idea I'd floated just before the breakup. After covering entertainment, nightlife, and social trends for years, I told my bosses I wanted to write a local advice column. Something focused on romantic relationships.

I explained that as a young person in Maryland, I'd read Carolyn Hax, of the *Washington Post*, and that when I discovered the world of alternative press, I'd fallen in love with the brilliance of Dan Savage. The *Globe* ran a few syndicated advice columns—*Annie's Mailbox* and *Dear Margo*, written by Ann Landers's whip-smart daughter, Margo Howard—but those writers had a national fan base. They were big names.

I told my editors that people in Boston needed their own, local advice column—a more intimate feature that would make them feel as though they were reading about someone down the street, maybe someone they knew.

I said I wanted the column to be written for an online community—with a robust comments section—so that it felt like a chat room. I would ask commenters to weigh in with their own advice to make the experience something like group therapy.

I was confident that I was the right person to launch the new feature. I didn't have any psychology degrees, but most advice columnists started their careers as writers and reporters. I was deeply interested in writing about the way people lived now—the expansion of Facebook, the dawn of text messaging, and the rise of online dating—and this kind of project seemed relevant.

Also, I'd sort of been an advice columnist for decades, at least to my family and friends.

In my youth, I'd counseled my mom when she started dating again in her early forties. She didn't have any single friends who could make sense of her post-divorce life, so it was up to me to help, and my mom listened as though I was the expert.

I helped her write dating profiles, first for the tiny print ads in *Washingtonian* magazine, before the internet, and then for online sites that made it much easier to find love in the suburbs. Once I was old enough, my mom's questions became more…specific.

I remember her calling me at college to ask whether she could have a man sleep over if she wasn't ready to have sex with him.

"You can do other things. You can fool around for a while and then just fall asleep," I told her, clutching my landline phone, covered in blankets in my freezing apartment at Syracuse University.

"I don't think adults sleep in the same bed without having intercourse," my mom said.

"You'd be shocked," I replied. "Get creative."

When I wasn't debating the rules of dating with my mom, I was watching my older sister. Whereas my mom had always been a hopeless romantic—a classical musician looking for true love like some Jane Austen character—my sister, Brette, who's more of a Bette Midler character, preferred big experiences and excitement.

From the time she was old enough to know what sex was, Brette had sexual chemistry with almost every human she met. She lost her virginity when she was sixteen to one of the hottest guys at our high school. They did it in her twin bed while my mom was sleeping down the hall. Then they went outside and had sex on our swing set.

Brette didn't care that the hot popular guy was only offering a one-night stand, and that her peers would hear about it and judge. My mom found out about my sister's virginity loss because Brette wound up doubled over in pain with a urinary tract infection. Even then, Brette had no regrets.

Counseling my sister was always different than advising my mom.

"Do you really need to do that?" "Are you sure you should be pursuing someone else's boyfriend?" "Was it really a good idea to sneak alcohol on that school band trip by hiding it in a bag of maxi pads?"

With Brette, I honed my skills at advising without judgment. I learned that recklessness can sometimes yield beautiful results. I learned that women can live on their own terms, without giving a shit about rules that someone else set for them.

As I got older, my friends benefited from my instinct to talk things through, although it didn't always feel like a plus. When one of my closest guy friends from college got married, I was asked to be a "groomsmaid," but I wasn't invited to the bachelor party. I asked why, arguing that my being a woman should not prohibit me from attending the celebration.

"It's not that," he explained, looking pained. "Everybody knows that if you come, we'll all wind up sitting around and talking about our feelings."

I let it go, knowing he was right. Sitting around and talking about feelings was kind of my thing.

♡

My editors were hesitant about the advice column idea at first. In 2008, they were slashing budgets; whatever resources and labor remained needed to go to important departments like the Metro desk and the Spotlight team.

But one editor of the website wanted to give it a try. The news business was changing, and he needed stories that would make people want to stay online all day. An advice column with a comments section was starting to sound like a good idea.

I panicked, because the breakup with Patrick had altered my brain. How could I be helpful to readers when it had become clear that I could no longer help myself?

I can attribute my rally—in part, at least—to Lisa, an acquaintance from work who was around my age. We had dinner one night, before the launch of the column, because I wanted to check up on her. Lisa's husband had died recently in his sleep because of some rare genetic problem that no one would have been able to prevent. Lisa had real troubles and had experienced genuine loss. All of a sudden she was alone in a condo in the suburbs trying to figure out how to start over without her life partner.

As I listened to her talk about her new reality, I had enough sense to feel ashamed.

"I'm an idiot," I told her. "Here I am, devastated about a dumb breakup with a guy I was dating for less than a year, and meanwhile, you lost a spouse. You're experiencing real grief. I can't believe I've been so stupid."

Lisa's response shocked me. She told me I wasn't stupid at all.

"Sometimes breakups are worse than death," she explained matter-of-factly. "The pain of rejection is different, but it can cut much deeper."

Lisa told me she was sure that if her husband were alive, he'd want to be with her. The whole point of their marriage was that they never wanted to let each other go.

"But a breakup means that someone is content to live without you," she said, looking at me like I was the one who deserved pity. "Patrick is healthy and alive and chooses not to have you around."

It was true. Patrick was in Brookline, on that stupid beige couch, under that framed *Globe* Sports page from 2004 that said "Finally!" probably eating a peanut butter sandwich, not thinking of me at all.

"*Asshole*," I whispered.

The conversation validated all that I'd been through over the past year.

It also made me realize that if Lisa could separate her grief from my experience, I should be able to do the same for readers.

At the end of 2008, I published a call-out for love problems on the *Globe*'s website and crossed my fingers that someone would respond. I freaked out when I saw the first email, shaking as I opened it, realizing that real humans—people I didn't know—were going to tell me about their lives.

A friend in the paper's design department made a logo—a

tiny envelope with a heart—and we decided to call the column *Love Letters*.

The first letter I answered—on January 22, 2009—was from a writer who went by "Desperate," who lived in the suburban town of Rockland, Massachusetts.

The entry drew reader comments within minutes. I was ecstatic.

There were a few trolls who used the comments section to make fun of the letter writer (or to make strange, non-sequitur declarations about Tom Brady), but they were outnumbered by thoughtful people who seemed to want to help. As the days went on and I published more letters, I'd ask, after entries, something like, "Readers, what do you think?" to make sure everyone knew it was a discussion.

Some of the first commenters who began logging their advice every day were Valentino, TheRealJBar, Sally, Alice, TrickyCrayon, and Rico, who only referred to himself in the third person (as in, "Rico thinks you should break up with your boyfriend"). The list grew, and I became a fan of commenters like Tricia, TrueLuv4Eva, MHouston, Two-Sheds, Bklynmom, Smash, and BackBayBabe.

I knew very little about who these daily commenters were in real life, but I began to fantasize. My mom—who'd just ended an engagement when I launched *Love Letters*—had her own theories. "What if Rico is a woman?" she asked, calling me from Maryland after she'd finished teaching for the night and scrolled through the comments section. "I think Alice is probably very attractive," she guessed.

I could tell the column was keeping her mind off her own breakup. Like me, she was trying to figure out where she fit in the world, now that her plan for the future—a life as a married woman—had faded away.

We were easily distracted, because within months of the launch of *Love Letters*, the number of comments tripled and then quadrupled. Most days, the website had a few hundred pieces of advice from readers within hours.

It also appeared that it wasn't just a local thing. Despite my theory that Boston needed its own advice column, people wrote in from all over the country, sometimes noting to me privately that they'd gone to college in Boston and landed elsewhere. As for the locals, they stunned me with their email addresses. Some came from places like fidelity.com, harvard.edu, and .gov. I was shocked to see that a few of the commenters were mental health professionals.

Those regular commenters kept coming back and developed their own packs of loyal fans. Letter writers would say, "I want to know what TheRealJBar has to say." To be honest, I wanted to know what TheRealJBar had to say, too.

People wanted my advice—but they also wanted to crowdsource their love lives.

I knew it was misery loving company. And yet, with the online company, I was starting to feel a lot less miserable. I didn't know where I was drifting, but I knew I wasn't the only person who felt unattached. My peers might be coupling up, getting married, having kids, and leaving me behind, but I had a new group of imaginary friends who kept me busy. They gave me countless problems to consider. With them, maybe I didn't need Patrick.

That said, I did hope he was reading.

DESPERATE IN ROCKLAND

(the first letter)

Q. I am seeing a man who has lived by himself for sixteen years. He has said he loves me, and when he is with me he is an angel. He is from Maryland, and when he leaves me he becomes distant and sometimes rude. He has even stopped speaking to me for six months because I made him angry. He says he wants what I want, which is a solid relationship, maybe ending up in marriage.

My problem is he does not like talking on the phone and, right now, that is our only option. He calls when he feels like it, and that may amount to maybe once a week. I want to know if this man has commitment issues and if I should run. I have tried to break it off three times, but he calls and we start talking again, and he does the same thing all over again. I like him, but I find it hard to get to know him. He won't even show me his feet. He was a serviceman for twenty-three years, so maybe that has something to do with his feet, but I am looking for a drama-free life and he is not helping.

—Desperate, Rockland

A. You've told us you feel like you don't know him. You've told us he cut you out of his life for six months—because he was in a bad mood.

You've told us you want marriage, but he won't show you his feet.

We all deserve someone who will expose their feet.

I get that this guy has a tough time with emotional intimacy, but his inability to include you in his life means he's wasting your time. Perhaps it's time to use your feet to walk away.

—Meredith

READERS? WHAT DO YOU THINK?

I totally agree with Meredith here. Your beau is downright cruel. If he is not willing to seek therapy (and I mean actually GO to a therapist, not just say he's going to do it), I would run the other way. Until he gets his act together, he is not dating material, much less marriage material. You deserve better than this! — MOVE-ON

He treats you like this because you're "desperate." If you have confidence and other options, he may act differently. Just stop being desperate…that's the key :-)
— PATSFAN0269

Run for the hills, woman! — J GILLY

Chapter 2

You Make Me Wanna Snoop

You'd think it would take a while—like, more than a few weeks—for people to trust a new advice columnist with their personal problems.

You'd think people would want to read a few dozen responses from that advice columnist, just to make sure she's not some self-help–spewing fraud, before submitting any letters of their own.

But within weeks of the launch of *Love Letters*, my inbox was full of notes from strangers who detailed steamy one-night stands, serial cheating, horrible first dates, and the overwhelming grief and financial devastation caused by divorce. It was as if people in Boston had been desperate to confess.

One of the first letters was from a guy who was ready to walk out on his fiancée. I got the sense he was telling me something no one else knew.

"I'm getting married next month, but I think I'm in love with another woman," he wrote. "I was always anxious about the engagement and upcoming marriage, but I took that to be cold feet or whatever. Then I met someone else who I connected with instantly, in many ways more deeply than with my fiancée. I haven't cheated on her, but I've wanted to."

The ease with which these letter writers shared their secrets and concerns was humbling—and jarring.

"You don't even know me," I'd mutter to my computer screen while reading submissions.

Of course, that wasn't entirely true. From my name, readers knew that I was probably Jewish. If they googled me, they saw a picture of a short, average-width blond woman in her early thirties. My relationship status wasn't public on Facebook, but my profile suggested I wasn't married.

Occasionally a reader would write in to ask me about my credentials, and I would tell them what I told my editors—that most advice columnists weren't practicing mental health professionals, because responsible mental health professionals don't give directives based on a four-hundred-word generalization of a problem. My column might be helpful, but the real mission was to engage and entertain.

That kind of question, though, led me to do more research about where I fit into the history of advice givers, and the more I read, the more I learned that it was a pretty Jewish thing to do. Ann Landers, Dear Abby, and Judith Martin, also known as Miss Manners, were all Jewish, which made sense to me. I wasn't raised with much religion, but I knew Judaism was big on questions and discussion. Happiness in marriage seemed to be a big deal for the faith. At least that's what I'd learned from *Fiddler on the Roof.*

Eventually I read about *A Bintel Brief*, the Yiddish advice column started by the editor of *The Forward*, and was shocked to see how the romantic quandaries of the early twentieth century were not so different from the ones I saw now.

As the column grew, I met readers in real life who asked whether I had a system for answering letters—how I chose problems and came up with my responses. I explained that I answered letters at random, usually in the order they were received, and that my opinions came from my gut.

I did have some rules, though, when it came to process. I learned I needed specific controls to come up with proper advice.

I experienced writer's block at the office—in part because I feared my coworkers could look over my shoulder and see people's private correspondence—so I answered all letters at home, in pajamas.

I also needed complete silence, no music allowed. If my favorite Janet Jackson songs were on in the background, I'd be more likely to tell people to get single. If I was listening to something like Bon Iver, I'd tell letter writers to do all they could to be held by someone who loved them.

Every letter was unique; people with similar problems always faced different circumstances. I told my mom, "No two letters are alike, and they all include such specific details." With every one, I started from scratch.

But when it came to those unique letters, I did see trends. One of the most common quandaries was the anxiety that accompanied the wait for "I love you." I received so many "When will my partner say 'I love you'?" queries in the first months of *Love Letters* that I could have published a spinoff advice column called "Those Three Words."

The other common problem—which was more difficult for me to unpack—was snooping.

In 2009 and 2010, with the growth of Facebook and ever-improving smartphone messaging systems, there were new and complicated ways to spy on a partner. I was shocked by the number of people who had no respect for their significant other's privacy—or, in some cases, the law. They broke into email accounts. They cracked codes.

My ex, Patrick, wasn't a technology guy, so I wouldn't have been able to do much snooping on him when we were together, even if I'd wanted to. He didn't have a Facebook account and used an early-model flip phone.

But even before Patrick, I'd never snooped on anyone. Part of it was that I believed in privacy, but I was also too afraid of what I might discover. I'd always preferred blissful ignorance to finding out someone didn't love me anymore. I wanted to pretend things were working even when they weren't.

I would have made sweeping judgments about these letter writers—the readers who were so quick to admit an invasion of privacy—if not for the fact that I was related to a snoop. That made me a bit more empathetic.

My older sister, Brette, whom I'd thought of as a mostly respectful human being, had become a first-time snoop at thirty-four years old.

After one intense decade-long relationship from twenty-one to thirty-one, which was followed by several years of hooking up with men (and a few women) around New York City, Brette—a casting director—met someone she wanted to date exclusively.

"I picked him up while he was manning a booth at the

Bryant Park holiday market," Brette explained during a late-night phone call.

"Of course you did," I responded, once again in awe of my sister's ability to turn any gathering of humans—including an outdoors crafts fair—into a singles event.

"He's a glassblower, and he's ten years younger."

"Of course he is," I said, because this was so like my sister.

"We met in the booth where he was selling his glass," she said. "I saw him and I had to have him."

Brette explained that her holiday market acquisition was a twenty-four-year-old named Ben. He blew glass full-time and often visited Cape Cod, where his family owned a toy store.

She described him as round, jolly, and with a big beard.

"Like Santa?" I asked.

"But Jewish!" Brette gushed.

Brette said that after meeting young Ben at the holiday market, she asked him to join her at a get-together she was planning at a bar in Midtown. He accepted the invite and met her at the venue, where they wound up making out in front of Brette's friends.

After that first "date," they began spending weekends together. He would travel from his apartment in the Hudson River Valley, where he had a glassblowing studio, and would stay with her in her apartment in Alphabet City.

From what I could tell, Brette and Ben never got sick of each other, even though many of their dates lasted an entire weekend. She was the happiest I'd seen her in years.

My mom and I had concerns about their age difference—specifically whether Brette should be spending so much time with a twenty-four-year-old artist who was nowhere close to settling down—but we couldn't help but love Ben once we met him. He was like human Xanax, the sort of guy whose kind smile could dissolve any of our bad moods or family bickering. We were in awe of his art, specifically his collection of intricate glass marbles. He also made complicated and colorful glass pipes that reminded us of Truffula Trees.

Whenever we all met up at Brette's place in New York, Ben would show us his latest creations. A pipe that looked like a candy cane. A pipe that looked like something you'd find in a coral reef. A pipe that looked like a cat's butt. (Cat butt pipes would become Ben's most popular offering. You put whatever you're smoking in the cat's butthole, just below the glass tail.)

"They're for pot," my mom would say, of the intricate creations, pretending not to be fazed, her smile tense. She'd always been a cool, open-book kind of mom, but because she'd spent her college years cooped up in a practice room at Juilliard, she'd never done drugs.

"I can recognize the smell of marijuana now," she'd tell me, impressed with herself. "It smells very sweet."

My mom and I loved to watch Ben and Brette get affectionate with each other because it wasn't your typical PDA. They stroked each other like pets and spoke in an invented language. Brette had always made up strange words and nicknames—her childhood name for me was Lush (rhyming with tush), which she never defined or explained—but Ben was the first guy who met her at her level of weirdness.

"Bee-bah, I love you," Brette would murmur to Ben, while rubbing his arms.

"Bee-bah, I love you, too, lady," he'd say in return.

With their round faces and curly brown hair, they looked like bear cubs at play—or in heat. Once, during a visit to New York, I walked in on them cuddling in bed. She was stroking his chest hair and called it "chest Narnia." She pointed to his nipple and said, "Aslan." I nodded and exited the room.

At the start of their relationship, Brette claimed she understood that the partnership might have a shelf life because of Ben's age. At twenty-four, he hadn't had many dating experiences, whereas at thirty-four, Brette had sown enough oats to choke a horse.

The longer they dated, though, the more she wanted him to be her real partner. Brette didn't know if Ben was capable of a long-term commitment, but she wanted him to try.

"But he's so young," I told her one night, thinking about how *not* ready for commitment I'd been at twenty-four. "Think about where you were at that age, Brette. He's a kid."

"I know," Brette said, with a sad sigh.

"Also," she added, "there's another obstacle. A big one."

"What?" I asked.

"Katya."

My sister said the name "Katya" the way Cruella De Vil says "the puppies."

Brette explained that one of Ben's closest friends was a woman named Katya, another artist he'd known for years. She was younger and thinner than Brette, with ivory skin, long brownish hair, and Cara Delevingne eyebrows.

Brette feared that now that Ben had a serious girlfriend, Katya would realize what she was missing and try to steal him away. Brette admitted that she'd pored over Katya's social media photos looking for evidence of a diabolical plan. She was also full-on snooping—checking Ben's texts and Facebook messages for proof. This surprised me because Brette was nothing like my friends and readers who played detective with the people they dated. I thought she was too self-assured—and maybe even too ignorant about technology—to take part in that kind of behavior.

I opened Katya's Facebook page, the part that was public, to see what all the fuss was about. A few photos were of her and Ben in outdoorsy locations. They looked like pals, smiling with their arms around each other.

But the images didn't put Brette at ease. They made her feel old and temporary. She stared at Ben in the photos, imagining a thought bubble over his head that said, "Now that I've learned my lessons with Brette, I'm confident enough to finally pursue the love of my life, Katya."

"I don't mean to be a jerk," I told Brette, "but Ben is not, like, Ryan Gosling or anything. He's a great guy, but I don't see women falling at his feet. I don't understand why you think Katya—or anyone else for that matter—would be desperate to lure him into bed or steal him away."

Brette sighed through the phone, like I had said something very stupid.

"Fat Jewish guys are *in* right now, Meredith!" she yelled. "All of these Judd Apatow movies! Everybody wants a big, funny Jewish guy who smokes pot and blows glass! Ben *is* Ryan Gosling right now. Ben!"

"I see," I responded, trying to remember the rant word for word so I could tell my mother about it later.

It was difficult for me to fully understand Brette's concerns because I never feared the Katyas of the world. It's not that

I was too self-confident to get jealous; it was more that guys tended to break up with me for *nobody*.

Patrick was content to start over alone. Same with my college boyfriend, who just wanted to be done with our relationship.

I told Brette that she shouldn't worry about Katya because Ben had known her for the better part of a decade. If they'd wanted to sleep together, they would have by now.

"Think about Pete," I told Brette, referring to my sportswriter friend, whom I'd met when I was eighteen, when I first arrived at college. "I've known Pete for years. He's an attractive guy who means a lot to me, but I've never thought about being with him like that. I'm not going to wake up one day and suddenly be attracted to Pete. Maybe Ben is Katya's Pete."

"To be honest," Brette said, "I've never understood why you haven't had sex with Pete. I'd *absolutely* have sex with Pete. I think you *should* have sex with Pete."

"But I really don't want to," I told her. "Just like Ben doesn't want to have sex with Katya. Some people don't have the desire to have sex with everyone in their lives."

"That's stupid," Brette said, and then proceeded to name all the people in my life she'd want to sleep with if she were me. My married work friend, Mark. My friend Tito from college. My friend Adam, who's in a band.

I told Brette she was projecting her own desires onto Ben. She might be the kind of person who walks into a social event and sizes up every guest as a potential sexual partner, but many people aren't like that. Certainly not Ben, who seemed more like me.

When I arrive at a party, the first thing I size up is the food. Is there cheese? What is the cupcake situation?

"If anyone's going to cheat, it's *you*," I told Brette. "You're the one who wants to make a move on everyone you meet. You're the one who has to manage your impulses in order to be faithful to Ben."

"True," Brette said.

But even though she understood my point, my sister's jealousy kept getting the best of her. The more she grew to care for Ben, the more she turned to Facebook for new clues about Katya.

She snooped again and again, waiting to find the inevitable betrayal.

Based on what I found in my column's inbox, it seemed that people like Brette were everywhere, all of them seeking to solve some relationship mystery, even if they didn't know what it was.

Most of my letter writers were more sophisticated about their snooping than my sister. Whereas Brette simply grabbed Ben's phone or computer while he was busy blowing glass, relying on saved passwords to check his messages, my readers hacked profiles like the Simon Pegg character did in *Mission Impossible*. A few implied they were addicted to snooping and would read a partner's messages every few hours without them knowing.

One letter writer confessed to checking his girlfriend's email, using language that made him sound like some sort of operative. He didn't seem to understand that even though she was cheating, he had also committed an act of betrayal. "I ran a search for any dialogue between her and her ex. Needless to say, I found *a lot* of correspondence," he wrote, like he was the good guy.

Most commenters abhorred snooping, but one early contributor, Tricia, told other readers that snooping in her youth helped her learn to trust her gut. By confirming her theories about who was being truthful and who was spouting lies, she became confident about her feelings. She said she rarely snooped in the present because she'd learned that when something felt wrong, it probably was.

I began to understand her point. It seemed that for some people, snooping led to peace, or at the very least, the ability to ask the right questions. Sometimes it led to a breakup that was a long time coming.

That's what I began to tell readers—that snooping *is* bad—perhaps unforgivable. If you're set on doing it anyway, you have to think about why—and what made you hit that wall.

In the end, that's how snooping helped my sister.

After logging into Ben's Facebook account and reading his private messages over and over, Brette was forced to admit that Ben's relationship with Katya was platonic. All she found were benign, kind messages, and based on what she read, Katya had never tempted him to stray.

The more important truth, though, was that the lack of evidence of cheating didn't put Brette at ease, because like most of my snooping letter writers, my sister was worried about something bigger, something that went far beyond Katya.

Katya represented youth and infinite possibility—all of the things Brette knew Ben would be giving up to be with her. Katya was still wandering the world, like Ben, while Brette was ready to nest.

"You do realize that Katya has nothing to do with this," I told Brette, who admitted that she still felt unsettled after so many snoops. "You're just worried that Ben won't be able to commit because he's twenty-four. That's what's really going on here."

"I know," Brette said, sounding defeated.

"There's no way to know the future," I told her.

"You're right," she said.

"If you love him, all you can do is see if he keeps showing up."

"Yeah," she said, disappointed, because pretending it was all about Katya was a lot less scary.

SEEKING PERMISSION TO SNOOP

Q. I have been dating this guy, "Dave," for a little over a month now. My problem is that I'm having a tough time trusting him. He's absolutely amazing, and we have a great time together. We live about thirty minutes away from each other and he comes to my place about three times a week because it's an easier commute. We have agreed not to see other people.

Here's my problem: After our first date, he made a mistake and kind of took off for a few weeks without any type of communication. He basically dropped me. He apologized for this a few weeks later, and I decided to give him another chance. I'm happy I did because now it's great.

He didn't make excuses—he basically said he was an idiot for doing it and he understood that he may have ruined things, but never really gave me a reason why. Fast-forward to now. I still have this nagging feeling that I need to check up on him, and I have basically been forcing myself not to check his phone for something else going on. I should probably back up and tell you that I was in a very serious relationship before this for four years where I thought I was in something good (living together for three years), and then I was blindsided by a breakup. Two weeks later my ex got engaged to someone he had been talking to behind my back.

I'm over my ex and happier with my life than I have ever been. I know my need to check up on Dave probably has everything to do with my feelings about being burned, but if I have this weird feeling about it, I feel like I need to check things out for myself so I don't drive myself insane worrying that he's talking to another person. Is it okay to snoop a little on his phone or am I being the crazy girl?

—Possibly Crazy, Please Help!

♡

A. It's not okay to check Dave's phone. You get no snooping pass from me.

It's also not okay to expect Dave to be super committed right now because you've only been together for about a month. It's fine that you guys decided to be exclusive, but you can't pretend there's a deep level of intimacy here.

Instead of obsessing over Dave's phone and the potential for infidelity, try focusing on how it feels to get to know him. As the weeks pass, are you more confident about the relationship? Do you know more about Dave's world? Are you having fun? You have to give this time to grow. Remember that everyone feels a little insecure at the start of something new.

Also, please let go of what happened after the first date. Dave didn't owe you anything back then, and sometimes it takes a while to get things going. Don't force him to make up for that onetime communication gap by making promises he can't keep.

—Meredith

READERS? WHAT DO YOU THINK?

You need to break up with him. You are going to snoop eventually, and you will find something that you will consider to be very, very bad. Like maybe he went on a few dates with someone else during this "disappearing" period, and you are going to view it as cheating or something else ridiculous. Just end it now.
— ALMIGHTYZEESUS

If you feel the need to snoop, you are either in the wrong relationship or not ready for one. This relationship is a month old and you should be deliriously happy at this point.
— ASH

The thing is, if you indulge this weird feeling, you won't be checking just once. You'll have unleashed the Kraken, and this will become your way of operating in the context of dating and relationships. — KAYTI

No, you can't snoop. He's not your ex. *Yet.* — WIZEN

CHECKING HIS GMAIL

Q. I really enjoy your column. I hope you (or perhaps Rico or Hoss) may be able to provide a bit of helpful insight.

I'm writing to you because I'm going through the worst breakup of my life. I really feel like my world has ended and I have no idea what to do.

My boyfriend of four-plus years took a job in Indonesia because it was a great opportunity for his career. He is a bit younger than me—I'm twenty-eight and he is twenty-five. Although it seemed impossible at first, we maintained a long-distance relationship. We talked on Skype and on the phone every day. Up until a month ago, we were madly in love and happy. Then out of nowhere he broke up with me. Over email.

I was shocked, saddened, and completely heartbroken. Unbeknownst to my ex, I have his Gmail password. I may or may not check his email then mark the messages I've read as "unread" (which is a trick I bet most readers aren't aware of). I'm finding non-sent letters to me in his Drafts, emails to and from other girls.

I know this is a horrible thing to do and is a huge breach of his trust, yet I have no idea how to stop myself. It's ruining my life. How do I ever move on? Has anyone else ever done something like this?

—My Heart Is in Indonesia, Swampscott

A. 1. We must stop checking the Gmail, yes? It's an invasion of privacy. But more importantly, it's messing with your head. If you don't have the self-control to stop, email him and ask him to change his password. I know that sounds nuts, but I'm not worried about what he thinks—I'm worried about how you feel. The Gmail stops today.

2. He's twenty-five and across the world; it's not shocking that this didn't work out. It doesn't mean he didn't love you, and he probably did. I'm sorry you were left behind and that he dumped you by email (not that a Skype dumping would have been much better).

3. You're twenty-eight. You're young enough to have new experiences, but old enough to know what makes you happy. Why not focus on the life you have here? Make it great. Make something that's all yours. Allow yourself to be miserable for a bit and then pick up the pieces.

4. People are going to tell you that you're batty for checking the Gmail. They'll be right, for the most part. But so many of us have been there. So many of us have googled more than we should. Maybe we've "accidentally" driven by an apartment or peeked at a text meant for someone else. We've all had a low moment. You're having yours. You can forgive yourself, but make it stop. There's nothing for you in his inbox.

—Meredith

READERS? WHAT DO YOU THINK?

You've gotten a confession out and I can gladly confirm that you are indeed a member of the human race. As our astute hostess pointed out, we've all had premeditated loss-of-control moments in which we've snooped on some level. That being said, you will find out, as I and many countless others have, that [snooping] is an exercise in futility. Stop checking his Gmail. Stop cold turkey. You are only extending and aggravating the pain and heartache. Don't beat yourself up over it or feel guilty for it. Just stop doing it. Accept that it was silly to keep checking his email and be done with it. — HOSS

Unbelievable turds, spies, eavesdroppers. No, we haven't all done it. That's what's wrong with this society. — MIKE

I have learned the hard way never to check the email of a current boyfriend or ex. You are NEVER going to like what you find. I found out my bf was living a double life. Our relationship ended months later. Ignorance is bliss. — TBRUSCHIFAN64

Chapter 3

The Rachels

Before I met Patrick, I had a long-term partner named Jess.

It wasn't a romantic relationship; technically, Jess was just my roommate.

But it was more than that—and more than a friendship—because we shared *everything*. We planned meals and vacations together. We knew each other's families, and probably used each other's toothbrushes.

At the time, I didn't know about the term "Boston marriage"—the label (possibly inspired by Henry James and written about by Rebecca Traister) for women living together as partners—but that's what we were, for six years.

Some people said Jess looked like Alicia Keys, but my sister, a casting director, agreed with me that a better match was Bianca Lawson, who played another slayer, Kendra, on *Buffy*. That casting was appropriate because I always believed that Jess and I were the slayers of something.

Jess's expertise was design, so our apartments always looked fancy, even when we were broke. She always made things smell nice. She knew how to keep plants alive.

Our favorite thing to do was to spend money we didn't have on shrimp tempura rolls, which we ate while watching *Law & Order* marathons on the USA Network, even on the sunniest weekend days.

"We should probably go outside and do something," one of us would mumble.

"Yeah, probably," the other would answer, not moving.

Sometimes we'd communicate in Lennie Briscoe one-liners.

"There's no such thing as hooker-client confidentiality," I'd say.

"Crouching tiger, hidden student," Jess would respond.

After many years of bad dates and romantic disappointments—including the guy who peed in jars because he was too lazy to walk to the bathroom—Jess met a man who worked as an executive at a local caramel company. He was special—something more. I liked him a lot, and he seemed to understand and respect my place in Jess's world. She moved in with him, and they got married on Boston Common not long after Patrick and I broke up. Jess was pregnant weeks after the wedding.

I was thrilled for her and learned that I didn't mind living alone. At thirty-one, I moved into a 700-square-foot condo, which I'd secured without any savings by qualifying for one of the last questionable loans before the Big Short. I found a new routine and realized how great it was to be able to sit on the toilet with the door open so I could better hear the television, or blast George Michael's *Listen Without Prejudice* at full volume without worrying that Jess might be trying to sleep.

The thing I missed, though, was spontaneous companionship.

I needed more friends who had nothing better to do than to hang out whenever I felt like it. I needed people who could get excited about making day-of plans to grab Indian food and see something like *Hot Tub Time Machine*, even though *Hot Tub Time Machine* only got two and a half stars in my own newspaper. Jess was still there for me, but not for that kind of last-minute nonsense.

That's when I began noticing the Rachels.

The first Rachel in my life was twelve years younger than me and an intern at the newspaper. She was a young woman in my likeness—a blond Jewish journalism student at Northeastern University, raised by a single mom.

We met at work, and I'm sure she thought of me as a mentor at first, but the more time we spent together, the more she felt like a cousin and, eventually, a friend. Her mom lived on the West Coast, so I invited her to come to my aunt Nancy's Thanksgiving dinner, west of Boston. Rachel and I would text late at night about guys she met at school and what job she might want after college. After moving in with a group of misogynist roommates one semester (one of them called her a "whore" for not taking out the garbage), sometimes she'd sleep on my couch for escape.

Once I realized how much I clicked with Rachel—and that our age difference didn't prevent us from understanding each other—I became open to other younger friends and all they could offer.

Another Rachel, also a writer, had moved to Boston from New York City after the end of a serious relationship. She was in her mid-twenties and trying to figure out how to make a life for herself on her own.

Rachel No. 2 was a few years older than Rachel No. 1, so she was that much more available. She didn't have homework and had more disposable income to do stupid things on weeknights. Rachel No. 2 and I would talk about whether she should get a cat (this was a concern; we were getting close, and I was allergic); what it was like to grow up as an only, adopted child; and whether I should join a new thing called Instagram (her answer, with an eye roll, was yes).

Soon enough, other Rachels appeared. One was a man in his twenties covering sports at the paper. I talked to him about his ex, and he told me about music, specifically Big Boi's first solo effort, and Solange, in general.

Another Rachel, this one eight years younger, worked in marketing, which meant she always wore very nice skirts and accessories. We watched the same television shows and memorized each other's favorite dishes at restaurants. She read romance novels on her phone and somehow described things as "amazeballs" without pissing me off.

A few of these friends were actually named Rachel (it was a popular name for girls born in the mid-1980s), but "the Rachels" became my sister's shorthand for *everyone* in this new group of younger companions.

"Who's going with you to that show?" Brette would ask. "The Rachels?"

"Yes, a Rachel," I'd respond.

Sometimes I wondered what the Rachels got from their friendship with me. I had some life experience to offer them, and I figured they probably liked that I wasn't a direct peer who'd respond to their concerns with "me too." I also imagined I was a nice escape from other twenty-somethings who, when it came to jobs and significant others, were sometimes competition. I'm sure they liked my pep talks, and that sometimes I would pay for dinner, no questions asked.

For the most part, though, they were the ones helping me. Despite all I'd heard about millennials ruining everything, the Rachels seemed to care about the rest of the world more than my peers. They gave great professional advice, always telling me to ask for more—and they were available, always green dots on my Gchat list when friends my own age were red.

The Rachels also gave me an incredible gift by helping me figure out why my younger letter writers were so monumentally miserable.

As it turned out, the most distraught readers of my column—the ones most likely to asphyxiate on their own cookie dough—were not people going through big divorces, or single parents trying to date while raising kids. Instead, the most dire letters came from healthy, attractive, employed, middle-class twenty-somethings who claimed their lives were THE WORST, sometimes just like that, in all caps.

I knew the Rachels could help me with this—because every Rachel I knew was miserable, too.

Sometimes my Rachels' brows furrowed as they talked about their horrible days, which never sounded horrible to me. They would text (because the Rachels did not call) phrases like "everything is the worst" after a bad date or a job interview. Sometimes those texts included emojis of knives and toilets.

My peers had their own set of problems that were arguably more significant (the ridiculous cost of child care, fertility setbacks, etc.), but the Rachels were far more devastated by their *potential* misfortunes. Rachel No. 3, for instance, sounded more upset about a confusing text from his ex than Jess did when her son was rushed to the emergency room with a life-threatening asthma attack. Rachel No. 2, meanwhile, wouldn't think twice about telling me she was going to die alone, even though she knew I was almost ten years older and still single.

"But...I'm older than you. Do you think *I'm* going to die alone?" I'd ask her.

"This isn't about you," she'd respond.

I tried to comfort her by explaining that I was an outlier, and that most of my peers had magically found partners by the time they were in their mid-thirties, but my assurances didn't help. Life was VERY MISERABLE. Toilet. Knife. Syringe emoji.

It was baffling at first, because from where I stood, my Rachels were at the perfect age to do whatever they wanted—even with their student loans. They could change their priorities at any moment. Dating apps were filled with unmarried people who desired them.

But the Rachels explained how all those opportunities made them feel as though they were living a high-stakes existence. They imagined themselves in a choose-your-own-adventure book that, at any page, could lead to certain failure.

Settling on one path meant missing out on another. Every decision was a small but dramatic death for other opportunities.

This had also been true for Jess and me in our twenties, but our fears of missing out were less intense because we hadn't grown up with social media. We didn't have Facebook when we were twenty-five—it was still open only to college kids back then—which meant that the only expectations we cared about were the ones we came up with together in our living room.

Rachel No. 1, meanwhile, knew the specifics of every lost opportunity. Just before she was scheduled to graduate from college, she fell in love with a Boston-bred guy—a musician—who had no plans to leave town. By opting to stay near school to let their relationship grow, she'd be missing out on launching a career in New York City, where there was better work. It was a timeless problem—should you sacrifice a professional move for love?—but unlike my contemporaries who'd answered that kind of question in the early 2000s without much context from their peers, Rachel was convinced that her choice could ruin the rest of her life.

This was something I'd seen in the column—something that made other Rachels miserable. It wasn't the choice that scared her so much; it was being constantly reminded of the road not taken.

Rachel No. 1 was haunted by the lives of others on her social media feeds. Almost daily while she stayed in Boston to save her relationship, another friend posted news about landing a New York job that Rachel thought would be perfect for her. Some of her peers were becoming big-time writers at twenty-two. A few even talked about book deals.

Rachel No. 1 cried about her decision to stay in Boston. She also cried when she talked about what it would be like to leave.

Rachel No. 2, meanwhile, maintained the resting face of someone who'd consumed bad yogurt. She couldn't pin her constant bad mood on anything specific, but in her mid-twenties, she found herself alone a lot—too much—and that was enough. Everyone else was *with people*, she said. She sought out adult coloring books. She felt disengaged and empty and told me she had trouble believing that any man she met online could truly mean well.

Had she made the right choice by moving to Boston after her breakup? Should she stay in New England or move to the West Coast? Like Rachel No. 1, she was forced to follow the feeds of friends who'd found different and maybe better answers.

My first instinct was always to tell the Rachels—and letter writers like them—that they needed to relax. What they saw as problems often looked like opportunities to me.

The daily commenters—who'd only grown in size as a mostly supportive, occasionally judgmental mob—were more aggressive with this sentiment and seemed to despise these young letter writers. Many of them believed that if your age started with anything less than a three, you couldn't even have a real love problem.

"Wait until you're in your forties—*that's* when it makes sense to feel lonely," they'd write. "Relax, *nothing counts* when you're in your twenties."

But when I imagined myself in the Rachels' shoes (vintage Converse), I knew they were not overreacting and that telling them it would all be okay would be no comfort at all. I looked at the feeds of their friends and got stressed out, too. I started to consider how my choices would have been different if I'd had social media as a basis for comparison.

Also, when I was honest with myself, I knew that every

decision I'd made in my twenties *had* been a crucial step to where I was now. I had a cool job at the *Globe* because I'd spent so much time in my twenties building my professional portfolio and teaching my editors that they could trust my ideas.

I had incredible friendships and family connections because I'd spent so much time in my twenties tending to them. The things I *hadn't* worked on in my twenties were now the voids in my life. I hadn't prioritized dating, so I entered my thirties feeling inexperienced.

Every decision in my twenties was vital—*everything* counted—and all I could tell the Rachels was that they were right to treat every one of their choices as significant. They were allowed to be stressed.

I began to pass that message on to letter writers, too.

I also assured the Rachels that they had every reason to complain about dating because people their age weren't the best or most accurate versions of themselves.

In my thirties, if I went out with a jerk, I could assume he'd be a jerk for the rest of his life. At twenty-five, though, evolution seemed possible. At the Rachels' age, when I was out with someone who disappointed me, I was tempted to ask, "But what if he changes? What if he grows over time? What if he's just an idiot *right now*?"

Single friends in their thirties and forties had a smaller dating pool, but at least it was easier to assess the options.

I committed to being a defender of the Rachels—the ones in real life, as well as the ones in my inbox—to anyone who forgot how difficult even the most familiar problems can be when you're young. The Rachels, with their end-of-days language, forehead lines, and furrowed brows, were grieving all that they'd never have—the jobs they wouldn't pursue, the pictures they'd never post to their followers—in real time.

I tried to remind my older, more jaded commenters that even if our problems were more significant, it was our duty to empathize—because many of us were Rachels not long ago, and some of us were still worried about being left behind.

These young readers deserved our empathy, our validation, and, occasionally, a toilet emoji. Just to let them know we understood.

DOESN'T WANT TO BREAK UP

Q. My girlfriend of two years broke up with me upon our return from a week-long vacation. I'm twenty-seven and she is twenty-two—and about to graduate college. She used the line, "I love you but I'm not in love with you anymore." It really hit me hard because I had no inclination that something like this would happen.

We both thought our vacation was great, but she says she came to a realization while we were away that we were best friends. I personally feel that she is so busy and has so much going on in her life right now with graduation—what she is doing next year, where she is living—that she panicked and for whatever reason decided I was the expendable part in her life.

I recently received a promotion at work and have to travel two to four days a week. We both admitted that this changed the dynamic of our everyday relationship. What I struggle with most now is how complete I thought our relationship was. I was very close with her family, her brothers who are my age, and her parents. We had a very open relationship where we discussed everything, and trust was never an issue.

I'm really torn because I told her that I wouldn't be able to be friends because my head and heart are still very much into the relationship. I feel like she gave up on our relationship too easily and has yet to realize just how great it was. As much as it hurts, do I just let her walk away? My heart says no but my head says I need to move on and if it's meant to be it will be. Please... I need advice!

—Help

♡

A. Hearts and heads. It would be nice if they could just get along.

I believe your ex-girlfriend cares about you. I believe you're both mature.

But you're busy, traveling, and pushing thirty.

You pretty much have to let her walk away; she hasn't given you any other option.

For the record, I don't think she sees you as "expendable." She just sees herself as twenty-two. That's fair, right?

Now all you can do is take care of your heart. Hang out with friends. Try to have fun on these trips. Prioritize yourself (meaning, if a friendship with her feels bad, don't continue it). And maybe try schmoozing with some twenty-seven-year-olds. It might feel good.

—Meredith

READERS? WHAT DO YOU THINK?

DO NOT remain friends with her. You can't do it; you love her too much. — JOHANNA

Déjà vu here. I had the same thing happen while I was just a couple years older than my girlfriend. She decided I was

the expendable part of her life. Bottom line, buddy, if she can't get it together enough to keep a relationship going while dealing with the "drama" of real life hitting her in the face soon, let her go and move on. That was the best thing I did—letting her do her thing and moving on with my life.
— NEO2112

The main problem is that you treated her like a princess. This probably means she took you for granted. Next time, just treat your woman like a person instead of a princess and you will fare better. — REFORMEDNICEGUY

WHEN DOES IT GET BETTER?

Q. Hi Meredith. I debated for weeks about whether to write in or not with my question because it seems so trivial compared to the other letters, and what I am anticipating for the advice almost seems as if it will be predictable (things will get better with time, you're still young, etc.). However, this has been eating away at me for a while and I am open to anything that will help me move on from this, so here it goes.

I was dating this guy for almost two years while I was in college. We were inseparable and were completely infatuated with each other. Looking back, I realize that I should have ensured that I had a life outside the two of us because when we broke up, I was devastated and completely alone.

This guy was my first love, we had talked about marriage and being together forever, and while I know that's typical with your first love, I really thought it would last. When we broke up, it not only broke my heart, it shattered it into so many pieces that I am still not sure that it's completely whole.

We broke up almost two and a half years ago. For the first few months following the breakup, we still talked every day, still said "I love you," and went on occasional dates. However, this was too much for me to handle and I told him that I couldn't do it that way—we were either dating or I couldn't talk to him at all. I did and still do not want to be friends. Since then, he still contacts me on every major holiday, my birthday, our anniversary, just to "talk," and we end up talking for hours. Our connection is still there, which is kind of unnerving. We have gone on a few dates in the past year and slept together once, which I realize is making it even harder for me to move on.

The problem is I feel like I haven't been able to find anyone else that I have that "spark" with. I don't feel the same connection with anyone else, and he's told me that he feels the same. I'm not saying that I want to be with him again but I want to be able to move on from this and find someone who won't break my heart and leave me. My biggest fear is that I'm not going to find something as good as what we had with someone else and that (as ridiculous as this sounds) I'm going to end up alone for the rest of my life.

I watch my friends with envy as they go out and meet new men and start new relationships while I seem to strike out repeatedly. Sometimes I feel as if I am watching my life pass me by, even though I go out and try new things and put myself out there. How do I move on from this? Will I find that spark again? How do I know that I won't end up alone... the eternally single friend as everyone else finds someone to pair off with?

—Scared, Lonely, and Hopeless

A. I lost some sleep over this letter. I think that's because... Once upon a time, there was a young woman named—well, let's call her Deredith Boldstein. Deredith dated someone very wonderful in college. Let's call him... Draco Malfoy. (There was a resemblance.)

Deredith and Draco adored each other. But for obvious reasons (age, geography, etc.), they parted ways after graduation. Deredith was expecting the breakup—she knew it was necessary—but when it actually happened, she was miserable. She felt scared, lonely, and hopeless. She spent much of 1999 and 2000 eating pizza and watching programs on a magical network that was known as the WB.

Deredith's friends didn't know what to do with her. She didn't want to date anyone else. She didn't even like to go out very much. She kept in touch with Draco Malfoy, but after every phone call and visit, she felt more confused, more rejected. Draco still loved her, but he was moving on, dating various muggles he didn't even like that much. Deredith began to lose faith in herself. She ate more and more pizza.

One day, Deredith woke up and decided that she couldn't accept what she had become. She told Draco Malfoy that as much as she would always love him, she needed to cut him out of her new life. She actually said this twice before, but this time she meant it. She took his number out of her phone. She took down his pictures. He respected her wishes by staying away. It was difficult for both of them; they missed each other terribly. But eventually the feelings faded. And by eventually, I mean a few years.

Breakups are weird. Sometimes the ones that should take forever to get over are a breeze. Sometimes it's a fling that knocks the wind out of you. Letter writer, your breakup was big. Not only did you lose the object of your affection, you made a major life change. You're not in college anymore. It's a whole new world and you're doing it alone.

Even though it's difficult, you must let him go. Once he's really gone, you can start the recovery process. Maybe he'll come back to you someday. I suppose that's possible. But for now, you need to learn how to be happy without him. Allow yourself to go through the mourning process. It's unavoidable.

As for friends pairing off while you're brooding and miserable—don't even think about it. Those people probably felt lonely and left out while you were in your relationship. This stuff is cyclical. There's no rush, and you're right, you have plenty of time.

The saying "time heals all wounds" should really be "an almost unbelievable amount of time heals all wounds." You just need more time and some real space.

If you're wondering about Deredith and Draco Malfoy, by the way, it all worked out for the best. He married someone else. She moved on and found sparks in new places. And because she was older and more settled when she found those sparks, they shined brighter. She'll always love Draco—and most likely, he'll always love her, too—but Deredith knows now that Draco would have never made her happy in the long run. I mean, nothing ends a relationship like Voldemort. She would have never put up with that nonsense.

—Meredith

READERS? WHAT DO YOU THINK?

You need to think of yourself as an addict, addicted to this person. You need rehab from your ex. Just as an alcoholic must avoid booze, a coke addict must avoid coke (and the people, places, and things associated with their use), you need to avoid this man, and people, places, and things that remind you of him. — JC

I agree with the advice Meredith gave except the "Maybe he'll come back to you someday. It's possible." You cannot let this possibility enter your mind. THIS is the type of thing that clogs the mind and puts you in fantasy-future-land. — AWS34

THANK YOU, Meredith, for sharing your own experiences (I'm pretty sure I dated Draco's twin brother). I read somewhere once that for every three months you are with someone, it takes a month to get over them. As someone who got out of an intense four-year college relationship, I can tell you it DID take sixteen whole months to get over that person and find someone new. — MARINAGIRL

Been there, done that, even bought the T-shirt. If this was the "first" big love, then you will love him forever. First loves are like that. — LINDA

Dear (500) Days of Scared, lonely, and hopeless, Waltham: Loved your movie. Soundtrack was great. Nothing better than a good Pixies cover, right? Remember when your ex—THE ONE—saw you in the park and said, "You were right about love. Just not about me"? That was a great moment. Why do you keep forgetting that? In the words of Frank Black: There is a wait so long, you'll never wait so long, here comes your man. — MISCREATION

Chapter 4

The Company Ink

I was hearing a lot about "work spouses." I knew the label was supposed to be a cute and harmless way to characterize a specific kind of friendship—the natural, intense coupling than can happen at the office—but referring to a work friend, even a close one, as any kind of "spouse" seemed wrong and misleading.

I did understand why people wanted to come up with a new term for their close office relationships. Those friendships were often more intimate, complicated to describe, and, sometimes, tricky to navigate.

I knew this well—because I had Mark.

In many ways—which I was soon to discover—Mark was the most essential person in my life.

I can't remember when Mark went from random coworker to the guy who knew the rhythms of my menstrual cycle, which celebrities I want to sleep with, and how my voice gets an octave higher after a second glass of Riesling.

The transition must have happened before I got my first

iPhone, because he's always been the first contact under Favorites. It goes Mark, Mom, Brette, and Jess, in that order.

Mark became a special kind of companion because of our proximity to each other in the office. Unlike my regular friends, whom I probably saw a few hours a week if I was lucky, Mark was omnipresent almost immediately. He was everywhere in my life, all day—sometimes the first person I talked to in the morning and the last person I texted at night. Some weeks, Mark spent more quality time with me than with his wife, Michelle. They lived together, but during their hours at home, they were often asleep or focused on their two young kids.

I remember the first time I met Mark, in 2004. I was new to the arts department at the paper and followed some coworkers up to the cafeteria for coffee. Mark was the tall guy from Northampton, Massachusetts, with pale skin and graying spiky hair that stuck up in all directions. Despite being forty at the time, which seemed old to me then, he appeared to have the energy of a teenager. He bounded up stairs and down the office hallways like he was dancing. He made weird noises to punctuate his statements. He reminded me of a more corporate version of Mork from Ork.

After a few months, we started hanging out after work. It became normal for both of us to check in via text on weekends.

Sometimes, in the middle of the night, I would check my email and see Mark's name, and then I'd have a dream that we were doing mundane things like going to the bank and grocery shopping. Even when I was alone, it seemed as though Mark was there—in the walls, in the air, whispering tasteless jokes and tapping his feet while listening to music at his desk.

I acknowledged to myself, as our relationship evolved, that I gave Mark a lot of time and energy—maybe the kind of energy that could be saved for a friend my age or maybe even a boyfriend—but I couldn't stop myself from leaning into the bond. Our connection reminded me of the kind of close friendships I'd had time to make in college. Our interactions were platonic and fun and natural. Who cared if he was older?

One of the first things I enjoyed about Mark was that he liked to do a dumb thing where he arbitrarily put the letter *R* into random words. He'd go to a Starbucks and order a "larte." He liked to refer to Ben Affleck as "Ben Arfleck." I don't know why that amused me, but it did.

Another dumb thing he did—once all boundaries of decorum were gone—was tell me which celebrities have big penises. He'd memorized a "celebrities with big penises" list he'd found online, so whenever I happened to mention a name from the list, like Huey Lewis, Mark would ask, with great excitement, his eyebrows high, "You know what they say about Huey Lewis?" and I would say, "Yes, Mark. Yes, I do."

Sometimes, when people asked about my strong connection to Mark, I told them I knew him in a past life—because I sort of did.

When my sister and I were young, we took classes at the Peabody conservatory in Baltimore. My mom hadn't given up on the thought of us becoming musicians like her, so even though we were low on money, she sent us to the lessons, considering them a necessary expense.

I was too young at the time to be trusted to walk around Baltimore by myself, but sometimes, after I'd finished my piano lesson and Brette was still with her oboe teacher, I was allowed to go into a few shops on my own, including a gritty record store on Charles Street.

I'd go into this particular record shop and challenge myself to make eye contact with the older guys who worked there, most of whom had Manic Panic'd jet-black hair and wore eyeliner like Robert Smith from the Cure. I got a prepubescent thrill from loitering in the aisles of cassette tapes and vinyl until those record store employees stared me down, and then I'd run out of the store, back to the safety of the conservatory.

It turned out that Mark and his wife lived in Baltimore during those same years. Mark worked in that exact record store and had jet-black hair and wore eyeliner. He was probably one of the older guys I saw and feared—and was thrilled by—every week.

Once we figured out the connection, I felt like we were destined to know each other. The Cure could write a song about it.

It's complicated, because at some point, when you're a straight, single woman in your thirties, it can become difficult to develop close platonic relationships with straight men, especially when they're married. Most of my straight male friends were grandfathered in from high school and college. It was becoming difficult to go up to someone's husband—even a coworker—and say, "Hey, let's go to the movies or get drinks." Sometimes people got weird about it.

But with Mark, it happened organically, and it would have been a bigger effort *not* to be close friends.

He was there when my body rejected the many apple martinis I consumed at Lucky's Lounge on my thirtieth birthday, and I was probably the one childless adult guest at his daughter's *Harry Potter*–themed tenth birthday party.

One time, Mark and I got stoned in an alley near Boston Common and then went to see the James Bond movie *Skyfall.* I consumed a super-sized box of Junior Mints while he got paranoid. During the scene where Javier Bardem takes out his teeth and reveals that his face is deformed from cyanide, Mark leaned over and whispered in my ear, "Promise you'll never do that to me."

I didn't know what he meant, but he looked scared, so I vowed I wouldn't.

Mark's wife has always understood our relationship. Right off the bat, she was like, "Have fun with Meredith," because I guess our intentions (or lack thereof) have always been clear.

Michelle, who also became my friend, told me, not long after I got close to Mark, that when you have kids, especially in the beginning, you often wind up befriending other parents whose children know your own. Those people are nice, she said, but some of them aren't the companions you'd choose if it wasn't about convenience. She acknowledged that on paper, I wasn't the most obvious close friend for Mark, but in the same way we can't help whom we love, we sometimes can't help whom we like. If she was jealous of anyone, it was Mark. Making friends as a grownup wasn't usually an effortless process.

Not everyone was as open-minded as Michelle. Once Mark and I got close, I could tell that some coworkers assumed we were having sex. The people who asked about the nature of our relationship tended to be men around Mark's age, which said more about their desires than anything else.

"So...is it like...siblings? Like brother and sister?" one boss asked.

"It's a work spouse thing, right?" asked another.

"No," I said, annoyed because I was sure that if Mark were a woman, no one would pay attention to us.

But even Mark's son tried to put a name to it. He'd seen his parents with friends, but I was younger than those people and I didn't have kids, which made me different.

"Daddy, is Merevis your girlfriend?" Mark's son asked before he was old enough to pronounce my name. Mark's daughter, who's four years older than her brother, had an answer before her father did. "No," she said, "Merevis is Daddy's colleague. *Mommy* is daddy's girlfriend."

That was almost right.

It was my mom—who'd never questioned my friendship with Mark—who explained it best.

"He's just our Mark," she said, when I told her people were confused.

She added, with more thought, "You guys are also a little like Tina Fey and Alec Baldwin on *30 Rock*."

"Except Mark and I are both Liz Lemon," I said.

My mom agreed.

I know Mark probably skewed my perspective when it came to the many letters I received about workplace relationships. It was a big topic from the start—about thirty percent of all *Love Letters* entries in the first few years mentioned work in some way.

The easiest questions were about dating in the workplace and whether people should "dip the pen into the company ink." I usually responded "go for it," because even after losing Patrick and having to see him in the *Globe* cafeteria, I still thought office romances were worth a shot. I told readers that as long as they were respecting the rules of the human resources department, they might as well dip their pens.

I also knew the *Globe* employed many married couples who met on the job. Those people all seemed content, probably because they'd married someone with similar priorities.

The harder workplace questions came from people who were concerned about their partners' close friends at work, or their own blurry office relationships, assuming they were already coupled. One letter was sent by a woman who wrote in to ask about her husband's new coworker, who liked to text him late at night, long after they were off the clock.

"My issue is that this woman (who is single) texts my husband, 'Jason,' during off-work hours. Their conversations revolve around personal things, not work-related topics. Nothing incredibly personal, but it's still clear she's reaching out just for an excuse to talk. I realize that when you work with someone closely you'll develop a relationship and get to know them, but her texts are downright flirty."

My instinct was to defend this other woman because maybe she and Jason were super-friends, like Mark and me. What did it mean to be flirty, after all? Inside jokes? Comments about sex? Mark and I texted jokes off-hours, and some of them were about sex (usually about me not having any, after Patrick). With all of the hours we spent at the office, Mark and I needed humor. We needed to talk about Huey Lewis's penis.

Michelle understood. Or at least I hoped she did.

I told the letter writer she was focusing on the wrong problem. "It sounds like the real issue here is the amount of time your husband spends on his phone. Is Jason paying attention to these texts when he should be engaged in conversation with you?"

For the record, I knew that sometimes I was too defensive of these workplace friendships. I knew that Mark and I might be an exception to the rule and that many "work spouse" couplings did turn into affairs.

I tried to figure out the line for my readers.

The big thing I noted, as I considered why Mark and I worked so well, was that he and I never used each other to escape our real lives. I liked Mark even more when I was exposed to his marriage and family. I loved how he talked to his kids and how excited he got whenever Michelle got a cool haircut.

I liked Mark *because* he liked his life.

He also joined my world, as opposed to being an alternative to it. Very early on, he met my friends and hung out with my family. He made jokes about giving me away at my wedding and said he wanted me to meet someone after Patrick so we could have double dates.

As much as I don't remember when Mark became the first contact in my phone, I do remember when it became clear who he had become in my life—what it meant to have a Mark.

During a January weekend, a year after I'd started the advice column, I took the train from Boston to Maryland because my mom was having stomach issues and was ordered to get a colonoscopy. My mom had avoided colonoscopies—even though she was about ten years past the recommended age to get one—because the procedure scared her.

Once, years prior, she'd been on her way to the hospital to get the test when she abruptly turned the car around, all of a sudden rejecting the idea of someone snaking a tube up her rear end.

But because of her new symptoms, she couldn't avoid the test any longer. She asked me to travel to Baltimore to take her to the appointment. Mark helped me keep up at work while I was gone.

I drove my mom to the doctor's office and made her listen to my iPod, which I'd loaded with her favorite Sting songs to soothe her before the procedure. Her eyes were shut tight while she sat in that waiting room, her fingers clutching the tiny old Apple device.

"What if it's something bad?" she whispered.

"It's not," I told her, trying to get her to focus on *Ten Summoner's Tales*. "People have stomach issues all the time. It's probably a polyp. A hemorrhoid. We all get the 'roids. Avoid the Roid!"

"Okay," she said, not laughing.

The doctor—who happened to be the father of one of my old schoolmates—found me in the waiting room about a half hour after the procedure. He was holding a picture of my mother's insides and his expression was grim.

"Meredith, we've finished the colonoscopy."

He sat down next to me and pointed to the image, his finger on a pink area near another pink area that looked like construction insulation. "This right here—this large area—this is cancer," he said. "It's not confirmed, but, Meredith, I've been doing this a long time. This is colorectal cancer."

Then he said about fifteen other things about how we needed to set up appointments for scans, and how my mom didn't know the diagnosis yet because she was just waking up. He said I should call Brette and make a plan.

"I'm sorry," he said.

I remember moving my legs, which felt like stilts, out into the hallway, and then calling Brette, only to get her voicemail. Voicemail over and over.

My next instinct was to call Jess, but I wasn't ready for that. Telling her my mom had cancer would frighten her, and then we'd both be scared, and I didn't know where we'd go from there.

For a split second I thought to call Patrick, but he wasn't my person for this kind of thing anymore. He never really was, even when we were dating.

My real practical emergency contact was Mark.

When you work closely with someone, they know your every move and what you need to accomplish each day. Mark was the only person who understood all of my hourly needs and obligations. That meant he was the best person to talk me through the next scary moments of my life. How would this work? Where were the best doctors? What if the cancer had spread? What if this was really bad?

For a minute or two, Mark and I were the only people in the world, besides the medical staff, who knew the diagnosis. I don't remember what I told Mark or how he responded, but I do remember feeling stronger when I heard his voice.

It was clear that whatever happened next, he was with me. I

squatted in the hospital hallway talking—not to someone who felt like a spouse, an officemate, or a friend, but to someone who was . . . Mark.

We were doing what we did best, devising a plan and tackling our to-do list, one task at a time.

I'M HIS "WORK WIFE"

Q. I'm forty-two years old and happily married with two small kids. I work full-time and enjoy my job. I've been at this job for about three years and have made a good friend who happens to be a guy who's about my age, my peer in terms of status here, who is married with a child—I'll call him Steve.

Steve is a great guy. My best friend here at the office. But lately he's been getting weird. He calls me his "work wife," he asks for hugs all the time (I tell him no each and every time he asks), he's started taking "surprise" photos of me with his cell phone, and now he's calling me on my cell phone after hours to talk about non-work stuff. My husband only knows about the after-hours calls, and that's making him jealous enough. If I told my husband about the other stuff, he'd freak out.

I love my husband. I know Steve's marriage is sometimes troubled, but, from my side, there's absolutely no possibility or interest in being anything more than Steve's work buddy. I have two questions: Do I say something to Steve? If so, what? I don't want to lose my best friend at work. And do I tell my husband or just deal with this and not torture him?

—Work Wife?? Not!, Lexington

A. Yikes. I think the "work wife" talk can be fine, for the most part. But the hugging? And the photos? And the boundary issues? Red flags.

Weird, awkward red flags.

I know you don't want to hurt Steve's feelings, but you have to tell him the truth. Say (and feel free to practice in front of a mirror): "You are my best friend at work—you make this job so much more fun—but I'm weirded out by the hugs/photos. Can you cut it out with the over-the-top 'work-wife' stuff?"

Then, after Steve turns red from shame, you change the subject and maybe throw out an inside joke, something to indicate that you're willing to move on from this. If he's a good work husband, he'll want to know the truth so that he can fix this. A good work husband doesn't want to sexually harass his work spouse.

As for whether you should tell your husband any more than you already have... well, sure. He should know that you also see Steve's behavior as odd and that you have a plan to set some boundaries.

If Steve can't play by rules that make you feel comfortable, a work divorce is in order. But let's start with some simple boundaries and hope for the best.

—Meredith

READERS? WHAT DO YOU THINK?

"If Steve can't play by rules that make you feel comfortable, a work divorce is in order." HAAAA. Meredith is right. Set some boundaries. If he can't respect them he is a creep. — SITUATION

Just an idea…call up his wife, and make plans for a double date to go play pool and have a few beers or check out a new restaurant. Make a point of bonding with the wife. It should kill whatever fire is there rather promptly! It certainly worked for me! — MERILISA

Next time he approaches you for a hug, make sure you are holding a nicely sharpened pencil. When he comes in for the squeeze, point the pencil tip toward him. He will then impale himself with the pencil in the lower abdomen. — BAHHOO

SHE HOOKED UP WITH A COWORKER

Q. I think I made a BIG mistake. I am thirty-two and have been at the same job for a long time. Someone I have worked with for four years approached me a while ago for "relationship advice" regarding his live-in girlfriend of seven years. I confess that I had been attracted to him but considered him "taken."

Somehow (I know this is where I should take responsibility)

we ended up essentially dating each other after he said he was effectively finished with her, but they were still living together. And then we slept together, which is a big deal to me but seems like it is much less so to him. Then suddenly he stopped all non-work communication with me and that was that. This happened in April and we are both in our same jobs, which require multiple daily professional exchanges in shared spaces with other coworkers. I am left confused, hurt, and angry at having been treated this way. Short of job searching, how do I handle this hurt?

—Big Mistake

A. Focus on your after-work life as much as possible. If you have great plans at night and things to look forward to, your social interactions in the office won't mean so much.

Unfortunately, this is one of those fake-it-till-you-make-it situations. You just have to get through each day, try to smile, and hope that it gets easier over time.

I won't lecture you about sleeping with a guy who was still living with a girlfriend. I won't tell you that you have to be more careful with your heart. I will tell you, though, that when someone comes to you for "relationship advice," you probably shouldn't try to date them. That's my rule, at least.

—Meredith

READERS? WHAT DO YOU THINK?

I'd love to hear his live-in girlfriend's version of events. Did she even know they were "effectively finished" while he was living in the same house? Methinks not. — BKLYNMOM

"And then we slept together, which is a big deal to me but seems like it is much less so to him." Funny how that works out. It's almost as if this was part of his plan all along. — RICH1273

The company holiday party should be extra fun this year. — WIZEN

Chapter 5

Fangs

I don't know why I decided to write *Love Letters* five days a week. It was a lot of days, and a lot of letters. Sometimes I'd panic that I'd run out of material, but there were always enough problems in my inbox, and the commenters kept showing up every day.

The paper started publishing *Love Letters* in the print edition, as well. It was one of the first things the *Globe* "reverse published," which meant that the best letters ran in print a few days after they were published online. Each letter ran with my answer and five to ten of the best lines from commenters.

The frequent publishing schedule did help the column take off faster. Early readers, many of whom had nine-to-five cubicle jobs, told me that *Love Letters* had become a part of their morning routines. Every day, they'd get coffee, check the column, and email about it with a friend. That kept me going. I liked being like coffee.

The other good thing about answering so many letters—

more than 450 in the first two years—was that I was able to figure out what I stood for, faster.

Mostly, I learned what I stood against, which were self-help philosophies that involved dating rules, and generalizations about men being from Mars and women being from Venus.

I did my best to dispel old-fashioned notions like the idea that straight men and women couldn't be friends, which apparently a lot of people believed because a fictional character in *When Harry Met Sally* told them so. I also tried to poke holes in the theory that cheaters would always cheat, because I believed that people were capable of change, for better and worse. People in my life—everyone but me, really—seemed to be evolving all the time. Like Patrick, who I imagined was hunting for a wife, despite so many years of avoiding big commitment.

As an advice giver, I was getting more confident about my opinions on many subjects, and no longer feared letters that were outside my area of experience. I knew that no matter what, I could fall back on reporting, interviews, and research. I tried not to use language like "I think" and "maybe" in my drafts. I didn't think, I *knew*.

Except for when it came to porn.

I was still sometimes confused about porn.

I had no problem with the concept of pornography and believed that porn, in its many forms, could enhance romantic relationships.

I'd always liked porn a lot, myself.

I'd grown up watching old-school X-rated movies from VHS collections hidden in friends' suburban basements. I was very familiar with one particular film, which was an inventive take on Lawrence Kasdan's *The Big Chill*, featuring characters who gather to mourn a dead friend and wind up sleeping with each other during one memorable weekend. The female friends admit they've always had crushes on each other, a disclosure that leads to sexy consequences. Each character also has a memory of having sex with the dead friend, all of which are played out in creative flashbacks. (I have not been able to find this film since high school. If anyone has a copy, let me know, because I'd like to show my film-critic friends.)

I would mock the movie with peers when I watched it as a teenager, critiquing its questionable dialogue and no-frills set design, but I also found it arousing because it was naked people rolling around together, and that seemed like something fun to try.

That's one thing I knew about porn: It could be a turn-on, even when it was very, very ridiculous.

But when my readers wrote in about pornography, their questions were nuanced and dealt with complicated issues such as frequency of consumption and gender politics. Some letter writers were upset about how their partner's preferred porn portrayed women, while others believed their sex lives suffered as porn became easier to access on phones and laptops. I didn't know how to be the arbiter of who, when, and how much. I understood that a partner's porn habit shouldn't replace intimacy in a relationship, but I couldn't bring myself to make broad rules about objectification and escapism.

Part of the problem was that I had grown up in a household where escapism by way of two-dimensional men was part of the daily agenda.

In my childhood home, my sister and I had a list of crushes

who earned their place on the walls and counters of our shared bathroom. Next to our sink was a foot-tall cardboard standup of Michael J. Fox that Brette bought at the local video store when *Teen Wolf* came out on VHS. The tiny Michael, with his varsity jacket and hairy hands, greeted us every morning, and sometimes I would catch Brette making eyes at him and touching his cardboard stomach. An image of River Phoenix hung above him, the poster of his young face taped over the yellow floral wallpaper.

We didn't think of our pinup habit as a teen phase—something we were supposed to grow out of—because my mother also participated. She cut out pictures of the object of her affection, Sting, and hid them where we'd least expect them. There was a magazine cutout of Sting in a bathtub taped inside the cabinet where we kept the dishes. Every time I went to get a plate, I was greeted by a naked Sting holding a rubber duckie. For a long time, she also had a poster of Robert Redford from *Indecent Proposal* on the inside of her closet door.

But the main objects of our affection were vampires, which were a special category of men we used for sexual pleasure and escape. The immortal men were shiny and undead, and in my Maryland home, they were everywhere.

Brette started us on this path, first when she discovered an Anne Rice novel on our family bookshelf (she was partial to the ego and antics of Lestat, who might have reminded her of herself), and then with the 1985 movie *Fright Night*, which we rented from the local video store week after week.

The original *Fright Night* (it was remade with Colin Farrell in 2011) stars Chris Sarandon—the actor better known for playing Prince Humperdinck in *The Princess Bride*—as a lonely and evil vampire who falls in love with a young woman in the suburbs named Amy. In a pivotal scene, Chris Sarandon, whose dangerous vampire name is, somehow, Jerry, wears a very sexy crew-neck shirt and dances with Amy in a nightclub. Amy is drawn in by his gaze and sways from side to side, entranced, as Jerry touches her butt. She also shimmies to the floor and puts her face in front of his pants. I found that specific scene to be quite erotic when I was young. Even then I knew I longed to dance with a vampire like that. That's what sex probably was, in my mind—dancing in front of an attractive man's pants.

(You can find that particular scene on YouTube by googling "Fright Night" and "sexy dancing" and "club scene.")

Brette and I watched that dance over and over, and I'd get lightheaded as Chris Sarandon watched us—because he was *watching us*—while slinking across the dance floor.

It was like the money shot of a porn, and we knew what to do. Rewind, repeat. Rewind, repeat.

From *Fright Night* we moved on to 1987's *The Lost Boys*, a movie featuring teenage vampires on sexy motorcycles, and when I got older, I found *Buffy* on my own.

Then one day my mom called from Maryland and told me about something new.

"You have to see *Twilight*," she said, almost panting through the phone.

"Eh," I responded. "I think that's a kid thing."

I'd heard of the *Twilight* books and the first film, which was new in theaters, but it seemed silly. All I remembered from the trailer was that the guy had fancy hair.

"It's not just a kid thing," my mom said, "it's a big deal."

"Plus," she added, her voice low, "it's *piano teacher porn.*"

"Piano teacher porn?"

I could hear piano in the background of the phone call, as always. My mom often called me for a quick chat while her students warmed up for lessons in her "teaching studio," also known as our living room. These conversations were always set to the slow and punishing soundtrack of Hanon warmup exercises and repeating scales.

"The story," my mom told me, over the loud piano drills, "is about a sexy young vampire, Edward Cullen, who plays the piano. Because of the books and the movie, all of my students are desperate to play Debussy because Edward Cullen *loves* Debussy. They all suddenly think Debussy is *cool.* I'm telling you, it's porn for piano teachers."

Intrigued, I made a date to see *Twilight* with friends. We got a little drunk first.

The movie started out okay, with pretty scenery in the Pacific Northwest.

But then, all of a sudden, I got *very* interested in what I saw onscreen.

"Hello," I whispered as Edward Cullen appeared for the first time, sauntering into his high school cafeteria, his hair standing up like he'd spent most of the 1980s stocking up on Aqua Net. He wore a crew-neck shirt, just like Jerry in *Fright Night.* It fit his shoulders just right. I wanted to touch them.

"Who is that?" I asked silently, to no one.

"That's Edward Cullen," the character played by Anna Kendrick said onscreen, as if she were talking to me. "He's totally gorgeous, obviously. But apparently, nobody here's good enough for him. Like I care."

"*I* care," I thought to myself.

Then I ate all of my Junior Mints.

"You were right," I told my mom later. "And it isn't just piano teacher porn, by the way. *Twilight* is *everybody* porn."

Twilight was already on DVD when my mom got her cancer diagnosis. That meant we could watch it whenever we needed to calm our anxious brains, sometimes weekly, sometimes daily.

Later, after scans, when we received the horrible news that the cancer had already traveled to her lungs, making her a Stage 4 patient, we focused on the release of *The Twilight Saga: New Moon* while Brette hustled to get second opinions at hospitals in New York and Boston.

The plan, so far, was that my mom would get a few months of chemotherapy to shrink the lung metastases enough to remove them. Then the doctors could remove the tumor in her colon. We hoped.

She planned to teach piano lessons through June but told her students she would retire at the start of summer. They didn't know she was sick, and she wanted to keep it a secret so they wouldn't worry. Her students were shocked by her abrupt retirement—some of them had studied with her for more than a decade—but they didn't seem to suspect she had an illness.

During those first few months of chemo, my mom called a lot—more than her usual twice a day—asking me to assure her that she would get better. All I could say was, "Of course you will," even though I wasn't sure at all. I didn't want to think about the question.

I changed the subject to *New Moon* a lot. We'd talk about traveling to Italy to find vampires as soon as she felt better. Later, when that sequel was released on DVD, we'd watch our favorite scenes over and over. Rewind, repeat. Rewind, repeat.

I'm embarrassed to think about how many times we watched the *Twilight* movies during the first few years of her illness. Sometimes, when I was alone, I'd keep the first film running while I did laundry and wrote *Love Letters*. It was my way of self-soothing; the familiar lines and happy endings calmed me before bed, and I'd sleep holding my pillow, pretending it was an undead seventeen-year-old centenarian protecting me throughout the night, giving my family eternal life.

I knew it was a lot like porn. Whenever I watched my favorite scenes, I could feel the release of dopamine in my brain.

Brette would tell you that she didn't turn to vampires to cope with my mom's illness, and that only my mom and I wound up falling into an abyss of immortal escapism, but that would be a lie. As my mom's treatment plan grew, Brette was hired to cast a small independent movie. She could have hired any sixty-something actor to play the lead but wound up offering it to Chris Sarandon—from our teen favorite, *Fright Night*—who was now about seventy. The veteran performer, who'd once been the subject of our earliest sexual fantasies, liked the script and took the part. Brette decided to spend *a lot* of time on set, even though as a casting director, her work on the film was done.

She said she stuck around "just in case anyone needed anything," watching Chris Sarandon film the same scenes over and over.

Rewind, repeat. Rewind, repeat.

I'd always believed (and told letter writers) that porn was a problem if it made someone less interested in the real world, but I was starting to think that sometimes, extreme escapism was okay. My version of porn wasn't just helping me deal with my mom; it was also magically erasing the lingering pain of a breakup. One night, for instance, my phone showed a missed call from Patrick. It was the first time he'd reached out since the breakup. Seeing his name made me break out into a light sweat.

What did he want? Was it a butt dial or did he need to tell me something?

Without my undead distractions, I would have stared at my phone with deep confusion about what to do next. Would I call him back? Text?

Instead, I ignored him.

"Nope," I said to the phone, because I was occupied by something with fangs. If Patrick wanted to talk to me, he could leave a message. (He didn't.)

But I would soon admit that my advice to readers was right—that my escapism had gone too far.

The turning point was when I went on a blind date with a friend of a friend. I didn't feel dateable with everything going on with my mom, but a friend suggested a setup, and going out with a single man my own age seemed like a healthy thing to do.

When I showed up to the dinner, I decided within minutes that it wasn't going to work. I was not going to date or sleep with this man. I wasn't attracted to him, and he seemed to be waiting for me to speak, which made me feel like I had to be *on*.

Also, his hair was unspectacular. He was not even wearing a crew-neck shirt.

I wondered how I could sabotage the date as quickly as possible. Blow my nose like a trumpet to give him a hint of what my sinus problems could bring in the middle of the night? Tell him that I didn't like small rock clubs, because I knew, going in, that all of his friends were in bands?

Before I could come up with a plan, the man asked about my hobbies, and I told him—without thinking—that I was watching a lot of *Twilight*. As if that were an actual hobby.

"I've heard of that," he said, taking a sip of beer. (I'd ordered a Diet Coke and a beet salad, a meal I thought would send a message that no one would be getting laid.)

"Those books are, like, really popular, right?" the man asked.

"Yes," I said, annoyed.

"I don't really know much about them," he responded.

"Let me tell you about them," I offered.

Then I did. I gave him all of the plot points up through the third book.

My date listened, responding with a few nods and "uh-huhs."

I called my mom on the way home.

"Did you like him?" my mom asked, as I sped down Mass. Ave., eager to get back to my television.

"No," I said.

"What was he like?"

"Um," I said, thinking.

The truth was that I had no idea what the guy was like. Maybe his name started with a *P*. I couldn't remember.

All I knew for sure was that he was too rooted in reality for my liking. He seemed nervous—not sexy nervous, but real-life human nervous—and humans weren't appealing to me anymore. Meeting him didn't inspire a dopamine rush. There was no scene from the date I wanted to watch again and again.

It was a revelation that inspired me to reread old letters and to heed my own advice. If I couldn't connect to other humans, I had taken my habits too far. The movies, books, and immortal characters had become the only thing that could turn me on or make me feel calm.

I had to force myself to watch and read less.

Just a little bit less.

I tried to see more friends, listen to music, and go to the gym instead of running to the vampires.

I even allowed myself to think about why Patrick might have called, because at least he was real.

HE SPENT A LOT OF MONEY ON PORN

Q. I've been dating my boyfriend "Chris" for 4.5 years. He's thirty-four, I'm twenty-seven. A couple of days ago I discovered that not only does he have a serious porn addiction (internet, cable, phone), but it's also put him $6,000 in debt. He's spent more than $10,000 on porn in the past 2.5 years. I told him that I needed a break to think, and I'm horribly hurt and confused about what to do. Prior to this, marriage had been discussed, but sometimes I wondered about it because of how he's changed.

Our first year together was wonderful. Then I went abroad for a year, which is apparently when the porn issue started. When I returned, I moved in with him and things just never seemed quite the same as they did before I lived abroad. He was very pessimistic, more unsure of himself than before, and we'd regularly (sometimes daily) get into fights over dumb things. His initial reaction to most things became raising his voice. We kind of worked through this, still having fun together, though our sex life was never the same (and now I know why). For example, I would try to get him to talk dirty, but he said he felt weird. Then I'd try to pounce on him when he came home from work. Nope. It turned into once every three weeks... while the entire time he was enjoying himself and talking dirty when I wasn't home.

Now that it's all out in the open, he's a mess because I told him we needed a break. This happened because we were looking to sign a lease for a new apartment and a credit report was needed. Slowly, over a day, it all came out. He kept lying, not laying all of it out there at once. He said he was embarrassed and ashamed, which is why he never asked for help before (understandable). Last summer I'd caught him using the "livesex" internet porn and he promised to stop, but apparently he continued. He kept using phones to talk dirty and cable movies you pay for.

He says he's going to go to therapy. I believe him. He says he can't imagine life without me. He always neglected to tell me these things before. He was always averse or anxious about marriage or kids or even a house. Now he's being very open with me and telling me he was wrong. Wrong to hurt me. Wrong to lie to me for two years since I'd bring up the lack of sex and he'd just say that's how he was. He says he knows I'm very upset and that he's going to try to prove to me that he can fix himself and then try to get me back.

I don't know what to do. We're not signing the lease for the new apartment. Our current apartment is month-to-month. I don't know if I should stay with him in the apartment and help him through this, move out and help him through this, or just move out and cut all ties. I'm very hurt and angry, but I do care deeply about him. I fell in love with the Chris I met before I went abroad and was left with just snippets of him when I came back. I want the original back, the one I always trusted with all my heart, but I don't know if I'm being delusional. I went home for a bit and I'm staying at my friend's while in the Boston area.

—Hurt, Angry, and Confused

♡

A. If you're staying in this relationship because you were in love with the original Chris, you have to let go. Original Chris is long gone. He existed for almost a year and a half a decade ago, and you, my friend, have no time machine.

What you have now is present-day Chris, a guy who is dealing with a serious addiction to internet pornography. He's a guy who lost your trust and was more interested in live sex chats than the real live sex he could have been having in your bed.

The best-case scenario here is that he gets the help he needs and gives up the porn. But even if that happens, the addiction and the aftermath will still be a part of your history.

Couples can get through this, and it's possible he'll find the control he needs and evolve into someone who can be a wonderful partner. But you need to consider what you really want. You were happy with him for a year, and then it was a struggle. Knowing that you'll never go back to the honeymoon phase of this relationship, what are you trying to save? That's what you should be thinking about while you're staying with friends—whether the best-case scenario with Chris is something you desire.

—Meredith

READERS? WHAT DO YOU THINK?

Save yourself. He's sick and you can't help him. Plenty more fish in the sea and they aren't full of toxic waste, which is what porn is to the soul. — IHAVEMYHATS

Personally, I'd rather be single forever than share my life with someone who racks up thousands in debt having online sex with strangers and lies about it for years. — DORA79

I can't tell you whether you should stay with Chris. I can tell you that for this to work out it'll take understanding (without judgment) and patience on your part. It'll take honesty and hard work on his. Even then, there are no guarantees you'll get past this. You have to do what you feel is right. No guilt, whatever you choose. — TWO-SHEDS

Who doesn't get their porn for free??? — ASTRO-NOT

HE LOOKS AT REVENGE PORN

Q. My husband looks at porn probably every day and, no, I don't like it. Before you dismiss my letter as the same as all the others, let me explain. I don't like the fact that he looks at it and, yes, it makes me feel bad, but I've come to terms with the fact that I can't change it and have learned to live with it. However, I recently saw that he was looking not at regular pornography, but material made by jilted exes and hackers who film women and post private pics without them knowing it. I feel like it crosses the line.

I don't see much on the internet about women discovering something like this. Am I crazy to feel like this type of material is worse than regular porn? I'm deeply hurt by this and it makes me question how well I know him.

—Concerned

♡

A. What you're describing is "revenge porn"—images or videos that are posted without a subject's permission or knowledge. Yes, it is worse than regular porn because there is no consent. Yes, it crosses the line. It is horrible stuff, and these sites are often designed to scam people out of money (the victims can pay a fee to get the images taken down).

You're going to have to talk to your husband about this. Ask him to explain what he's watching and why. It could be that he likes the realistic look of the material—that the images are unaltered, as opposed to fabricated for his viewing pleasure. It could be that he clicked the wrong link and fell down the rabbit hole. Just hear him out and decide whether his explanation gives you any comfort. Find out whether he understands why it's wrong.

If a conversation doesn't put you at ease, it's couples therapy time. Not just because of the revenge porn, but because you feel estranged from your husband. You should feel like you know him and trust him. If you don't, the marriage doesn't work.

—Meredith

READERS? WHAT DO YOU THINK?

This is sad. Revenge porn is a real issue and a lot of women have pictures/videos of them posted online without their consent; those pictures/videos can haunt them for years and potentially ruin their careers. — CYBERSPECTRE

I'm sure your husband is probably just as "deeply hurt" that you check his browser history regularly, monitor his activity, and essentially disrespect his privacy. So choose your words carefully if you actually intend on approaching him about this. — MISSM78

I never realized what a sheltered life I had until I started reading this blog. I learn something new every day. — MOVA

Chapter 6

Behave Yourself

One of the first times readers really lashed out at me in the comments section is when I wrote to a recently divorced woman who hadn't dated in thirty years. She asked what to expect after being out of the game for so long, and I gave her some basic updates, like the fact that most people were dating online now, and that in some circles, bikini waxes were big. I also said this: "If you go online to date, you may notice that some men only want to date younger women. They won't even consider women their own age. Ignore those men. They are crap."

I wrote that piece of advice because of my mom's dating experiences. As soon as she started seeking love online in her fifties, she learned that men her own age wanted forty-something women—or younger.

It was already happening to my friends who were on Match.com and other sites. Thirty-something single women I knew were being contacted by fifty-year-olds, while being ignored by their peers. It was one of the many reasons I wanted to avoid online dating myself.

Some readers did not like what I had to say to that letter writer. They thought it was okay for men (or maybe for people, in general) to prefer and seek out younger partners. They considered it a matter of taste; some people don't like blondes, some people don't like partners over forty, etc.

One commenter said, "Why would you label these men as crap? They are being honest about what they want and expect—I'd think you would find that refreshing…The label seems too judgmental."

The sticking point seemed to be the word "crap," so I made a note to myself to stop name-calling in the future.

I still believed that those men were crap, though. I couldn't figure out why I should have to empathize with anyone who went out of their way to avoid spending time with people their own age.

But then I met Harry's brother.

Harry was a younger friend from college who I'd always thought was very attractive.

He had the sweet face of the lead singer in a boy band and sometimes called me late at night, after I graduated, for love advice.

I'd always known that Harry had a brother, but I didn't meet him until more than a decade after graduation, when Harry and his wife hosted a dinner at a restaurant in Harvard Square.

There were about a dozen people at the dinner, most of them

strangers. They were all couples—except for one guy in the corner, so I sat next to him. Together, he and I could avoid feeling like the eleventh and twelfth wheels.

It turned out that the guy in the corner was Harry's brother. He resembled Harry—they had the same skinny frame, peachy skin, and brown hair—but whereas Harry looked like the boy band frontman, his brother looked like the shy one. The poet. The Zayn.

I had mediocre expectations for the dinner, knowing I'd be with a table full of younger couples, but because of Harry's brother, it was a great night. He didn't know anything about my life, which was a relief. He wasn't like my other friends, who kept asking about my mother's health status, which made me anxious because I didn't have any answers.

Harry's brother and I talked about music and learned that we liked a lot of the same bands. We discussed my column, and he was curious about how I came up with love advice for strangers. It had been so long since I'd been around a guy who asked me so many thoughtful personal questions. I couldn't remember being with someone who was so funny—at least not since Patrick.

He asked me for my number. I put him in my phone as HB (Harry's Brother).

We made plans via text to see a show at the House of Blues a few weeks later. I drove, and at the end of the night, I dropped him off where he lived—which turned out to be in a dorm, at Northeastern University.

HB was still in college.

I will admit that I knew he was a student; at dinner, he'd mentioned transferring schools for a better experience. I figured, though, that maybe he was a few years older than the other undergraduates. I decided—or hoped—that he'd probably taken some gap years.

The reality was that he was barely twenty-one.

I quickly rationalized that it didn't matter. I didn't intend to date him. After all, maybe HB was another Rachel.

But he didn't give off Rachel vibes. Our night at the House of Blues felt a little like a date, at least to me. There was a meal and entertainment, and a lot of hours of getting-to-know-you anecdotes. There were a few moments that had me nervous and fidgety like I was on a date. I had put some thought into my outfit, which suggested that somewhere in the back of my mind, it was more than a platonic outing.

I told Rachel No. 1 about it, hoping she'd say it was cool that I was going out with a college kid. She did not.

"He's, like, my age," she said, addressing me like I was Amy Poehler trying to be the cool mom in *Mean Girls*.

"It's just two people going out to see music," I told her.

"It's a little weird," she said.

Then it hit her that they were both students at Northeastern. "I wonder if I know him."

For a second, I wondered if Rachel and HB would make a nice couple. Then I got jealous, which made me upset and confused.

Not long after our first outing, HB texted to ask if I wanted to see another show, and I said yes because I did. I did not hope for a hookup—my mind didn't jump to that place with him—but I liked how it felt to have his company. It was a safe date—because it wasn't really a date at all.

That second night we got into deeper personal stories. I

told him about my mom and trembled as I explained that the cancer was already in her lungs. Brette and my mom kept redrawing their plan to fight the disease, and I knew, from the looks on the doctors' faces, that our odds were changing.

I also told HB about how I sometimes felt like a single person floating in space. I explained that in my thirties, most of my friends were on opposite paths, with spouses and kids, and that I didn't know what I wanted instead of those things. I didn't know if he'd understand at his age, but he said he did.

HB then disclosed that he was also living in fear of an illness. He'd been diagnosed with a health problem—a heart condition—that involved constant monitoring. He wasn't supposed to drink and always needed a full night of sleep. The new friends he'd made at school were always drinking and not sleeping, so it had become difficult for him to find companionship.

I was ideal company, he said. At my age, I wasn't up all night, looking for the next party. I was happy to have a half a glass of Riesling at the House of Blues, hear a chill band, and then go home.

We kept going to concerts, and I started doing daily searches for local shows to find an excuse to see him again. With HB, I felt like a better version of myself, because all of the ordinary things about me seemed special in his eyes.

He said I was much cooler than the women he knew at school. I owned my own condo and read many books, and not because they were homework. My life did not require a meal card, and I'd been to Lollapalooza—the early ones with Jane's Addiction and the Beastie Boys.

Around HB, I felt worldly. I could never disappoint.

I began to feel a new kinship with the letter writers who only wanted to date younger people. Not-quite-dating HB made me feel like George Clooney. Being George Clooney is the best.

I liked that we were so focused on music, even in my car. Despite his age, he knew all of my favorite songs, which was odd because some of them were on the radio before he was born. I played him *99.9°F* by Suzanne Vega, thinking I'd introduce him to a new artist, but he already knew her best-of album. He was familiar with Jeff Buckley and early Liz Phair.

"Maybe HB is a vampire," I considered.

I was less familiar with the newer music he liked, so he educated me. One night he put on a song by Cold War Kids, a band I didn't know. He played me their song "Audience."

"You're going to love this one," he said.

I liked the cadence of the tune, and the lead singer's voice, so I downloaded the whole EP that night. It was called *Behave Yourself*.

On a long walk downtown one afternoon, HB and I found ourselves talking about *the illnesses*. He was getting tired of self-care and wanted to feel like a real college kid who could be more haphazard about his life.

My mom's doctors' appointments, meanwhile, were multiplying, and I didn't like that the surgeons and the oncologists seemed to suggest different outcomes for treatment. The surgeons gave good news with confidence. "We can cut everything out," they'd say, of her lung metastases, suggesting she might be able to get rid of the disease and live a full life.

But the oncologists? They answered every question with an anxious "we'll see." Brette and I had heard one frightening assessment from a doctor at Johns Hopkins. She'd told us, "Some people live three or four years with this!" As if only four more years with my mother was acceptable.

"I don't know who we're supposed to believe," I told HB.

"Also," I continued, "my mom has officially stopped behaving like an adult. She gets scared and cries, and then forces us to tell her everything will be okay. How can I promise that? I have no idea what's happening, and I'm scared to death myself."

"Whatever you do," HB advised, "*do not* google your mom's cancer. It will drive you crazy. If I googled my condition, I'd be freaked out all the time. It's better just to stay offline and not know all the ways it might play out." It wasn't practical advice, but I liked it.

Later, we bought tickets to see Air at the Berklee Performance Center. On the day of the show, HB asked if I wanted to stop by his frat house to hang out first. The "yes" was out of my mouth before he could finish the sentence.

I wasn't the kind of person who got invited to frat houses in college. I was a student newspaper geek, invisible to that kind of guy, or at least I'd assumed I was.

This felt like a weird chance to live someone else's life, to be the kind of girl who partied at a guy's fraternity, even if it was just for an hour before a show.

HB walked me into the living room of his frat house that night without embarrassment, maybe even with some pride. A bunch of his nineteen- and twenty-year-old friends were gathered in the kitchen, in dresses and tuxedoes, because they were on their way to a formal. I stared at their black-tie getups, my smile growing as I realized that HB was happy to skip this party—so that he could hang out with me.

"This is Meredith," HB said.

"Hey," I added, my voice confident, even though I felt a little ashamed to be there.

They eyed me with confusion and interest. Maybe I was his aunt. Maybe I was a conservatively dressed escort for hire.

We went into the basement and smoked pot. The frat house was a lot cleaner than I thought it would be; it was nothing like what I'd seen in *Animal House* or *Old School*.

Minutes later, my head in the clouds, HB and I walked to the Berklee Performance Center, a venue with ideal acoustics for a show like Air, and took our seats. For those who don't know, Air is a French duo that makes electronic music so dreamy that it served as the soundtrack to the Sofia Coppola movie *The Virgin Suicides*. Air is big on psychedelic swells.

As the music flooded the small performance hall, I inched closer to HB and imagined that we had magnets in our heads. I felt myself falling toward him, like I had no control over my body. Our knees touched.

In my weed-muddled mind, we were floating, both of us, flying high above a world where we had to wait on scans and tests and felt alienated from our peers. He tapped his knee. I imagined that if he took my hand, we could launch from our seats.

Not long after that night, I was out with my friend Danielle—a friend my own age—and we ran into HB at the Sia concert. This was before Sia was covering her face with wigs, when she could still perform in a small venue.

HB's condition was improving, and he was there with a friend from school.

Somehow, standing next to Danielle, HB looked much younger—like a college kid.

Danielle was cordial when she met him, but I knew her face too well. With one glance in my direction, she said, "Is this who you've been spending time with? What the hell are you doing?"

She said all that with one narrowing of the eyes. Or at least that's what I imagined she was thinking.

"This isn't like hanging out with the Rachels," were the words in Danielle's floating thought bubble. "You're not seeking friendship, you're looking for escape."

She was right.

It wasn't the only judgment I received. Harry texted me around this time, asking if I could get together with him and his wife.

"Sorry it's been a while," I said. "I've been so busy."

"You seem to have a lot of time to hang out with my brother," the next text said.

"Yes," I responded, because I didn't know what else to say.

From then on, when I got letters from people who limited themselves to younger partners, I didn't assume that they were crap. Sometimes I wondered if they were secretly miserable—or very scared of something they couldn't control.

My relationship with HB phased out without my having to put a stop to it, partly because he kept going home during school vacations and also because he was busy with classes. Before long, I saw on Facebook that he'd fallen in love with a woman his own age. She looked nice.

I no longer had time for HB anyway. As months passed, I needed every minute to work on my column, or to make plans for my mom to move to Boston after her first round of chemo and surgeries. She'd always hoped to settle near me after retirement, and we figured that whatever health care she was receiving in Maryland could also be carried out at Mass General.

I also needed more time for Brette, who considered herself to be our family's official medical strategist. I'd sit on the phone with her late at night talking about doctors. Sometimes I'd hear Ben in the background.

After much discussion, Ben had decided to move in with my sister. She was ecstatic that he would be with her all the time but was even more frightened of how devastating it would be if he wasn't able to commit for good.

Brette said she felt bad that I was going through our mom's illness without the support of a romantic partner, but I told her I was okay and that it was probably for the best I wasn't trying to balance our mom and a new relationship at the same time. It was mostly true.

On the nights I did feel alone, I listened to the soundtrack I'd made during my time with HB.

Sometimes it was that Cold War Kids song "Audience" on repeat. The first line echoed through my living room.

"Sunday nights that you want her—like velvet cake."

The lyrics took me somewhere I needed to go.

MY GIRLFRIEND AND HER "BLACK HOLE OF NEVER-ENDING EMOJIS"

Q. I've been seeing a girl for the past six months. We met online and things have been pretty good. She's a sweet girl—smart, fun, and open to adventure. But I'm starting to see some mismatches in our expectations of one another, namely methods of communication.

I'm thirty-three and she's twenty-five. My job has me traveling about thirty percent of the time, which to me is just perfect in that I am refreshed every time I get back from a business trip and ready to give all my attention to her. My girlfriend has been pretty cool about all the travel. The issue is what I can only describe as rated T for Teen. She loves to text all day, Snapchat, WeChat, Instagram, Facebook, Tumblr, etc. (you get the point). I love receiving thoughtful good morning texts, and I too initiate those, but once initiated I feel I get sucked into a black hole of never-ending emojis, commentary on the most mundane things, and pictures of her meals—and on and on it goes.

Sometimes I indicate I will be in a meeting, so please no texts. This is met with a flood of emojis and she will switch this up with comments on Instagram so she can keep me in the loop on her day. It has gotten to the point where instead of indicating I have to go, which will result in a deluge of "see ya" texts, I just clam up and don't respond. I mean, I don't mind the attention but I'm starting to see the age difference. I'm not built for constant contact.

She mentioned very recently that she feels I'm not

putting in the same effort, but I don't see it that way. I have been honest about my lack of social media interaction and that I'm just not into it. I don't have a Facebook, I stopped at MySpace years ago, and barely update my Instagram. She is still trying to convince me to give Snapchat a try. I haven't budged and it has been a sticking point in several arguments.

I don't like to feel obligated to be pulled down a rabbit hole of texts, social media contact, and comments in addition to all the things we do together three to four days a week. For what it's worth, the sex is amazing and time spent together is filled with good conversation and spontaneous trips. I think she is wonderful and the relationship could go somewhere, but what I am seeing shows that maybe the age gap could be a deal breaker.

—Stopped at MySpace

A. Have the talk again. Make your boundaries clear. Tell her that you're only going to text once or twice a day and that you're never going to sign up for Snapchat. At best, you can promise more phone calls. Talking is great, but social media? It's not going to happen.

I'm all for compromises, but this isn't the time to make promises you don't want to keep. Remind her that you have the same rules for everyone in your life. It's not as though you're texting friends all day but choosing not to respond to her food photos. This is just who you are.

Offer up more phone calls when you're on the road. See if that works. If not, it might be time to send her the Bitmoji that shows you walking away. Or the one that says "Game Over." I like that one.

—Meredith

READERS? WHAT DO YOU THINK?

She's a millennial. You're obviously not. You have two choices: Adapt or Eject. — HARRISBLACKWOODSTONE

She sounds sixteen not twenty-five. Act accordingly. — BKLYNMOM

:) :) :) :) :) :) — ALYSSAJONES

OUR FIFTEEN-YEAR AGE GAP

Q. I am a forty-five-year-old woman who has been in a relationship with a wonderful guy for a year now. Before meeting my boyfriend, I was a happy and busy single mother (my son is now in his twenties) and was not one to pursue a relationship. Between being a mother, socializing with amazing groups of friends, going to the gym, volunteering my time, and traveling (I love going solo), I never felt that I was missing anything by being single.

Now I can't imagine my life without this person. He is the

kindest, most considerate, fun, smart, compassionate man I have ever been involved with, and he makes me feel beautiful and loved every day. It also doesn't hurt that we have phenomenal chemistry and our love life could not be better. We have met each other's friends, family, and coworkers, and spend time with each other's children. My son gets along with him extremely well and I adore his children. Neither of us want more children and we both see a wonderful future together.

The reason I'm writing is that my boyfriend is thirty years old. I know the "age gap" letter is not groundbreaking stuff, but here it is anyway. I am the loudest "age is just a number" cheerleader, and our age difference in no way affects our relationship. What I do think about is "down the line." What will it be like for a forty-year-old to be involved with a fifty-five-year-old (eek!)? Will he look at me one day and think, "How did I end up with this old lady?" I know I am putting the cart before the old mare here, but I do think about it and would love advice on how to put it out of my mind and to hear about other people's experiences. I know that no matter what happens I will take it, because the time I spend with this man would be worth it, but advice is greatly appreciated!

—Potential Old Mare

♥

A. *"I know that no matter what happens I will take it, because the time I spend with this man would be worth it..."*

If that's how you feel, you have to make peace with the what-ifs. It's possible that the age gap will begin to feel massive, but maybe you and your boyfriend won't care. It's also possible that you'll take better care of yourself than he does, and that he'll be the one who feels like an old horse.

The cool thing is that you like him enough to imagine what life will be like with him ten years from now. And that's what you have to remember—that if you're still together when you're forty and fifty-five, you'll have a decade of history behind you. Those years will be more significant than new wrinkles.

Instead of guessing about all of the potential problems, just focus on year two. That's the only year that matters right now.

—Meredith

READERS? WHAT DO YOU THINK?

My parents had a fourteen-year age gap...Mom the younger one...running joke was she would be putting flowers on his grave long before he would on hers... sadly, Mom passed last year. And the ninety-four-year-old dad? Still kicking...— BACKBAYBABE

My mother was fourteen years older than my father. They married when he was twenty-three and she was thirty-seven. He loved and adored her for the entirety of their marriage. She never seemed older than him because she always had an optimistic, life-affirming attitude. — FINNFANN

I love that the Old Mare is asking advice from Old Mere(dith). — RICK SANCHEZ

Chapter 7

The Salon

My mom's treatment plan was a bigger—more philosophical—question than I thought it'd be.

It also had more to do with my column than I ever thought it could.

She'd been given two choices for chemotherapy, equal in their effectiveness, we were told. One kind would make all of her hair fall out, while the other would only make *some* of her hair fall out.

The catch with the second one was that she'd probably wind up with discomfort in her fingers. The doctors called it neuropathy.

I figured that Brette would be the first of us to weigh in on our mom's medical options—she'd been navigating her own Crohn's disease since her twenties, so she *was* the best at processing medical questions—but in this case, my mom was quick and assertive with her answer.

"I want to keep my hair," Mom said, determined. "I'll deal with the neuropathy. I can't lose all of my hair."

My mom's choice surprised me because her life revolved around her music. She practiced every day and needed to play for her students, at least until she retired and moved to Boston. Finger numbness—that neuropathy problem—didn't seem best for a piano teacher.

"You sure about that?" I asked in my advice-columnist voice, soft but skeptical. "Your fingers are your most important tools."

They were so important that my mother had always refused to participate in most sports, including bowling (the holes in the ball scared her).

"These are my source of income," she'd say when Brette and I were kids, showing us jazz hands. "I can't stick my fingers into a bowling ball. These fingers are how we pay the heating bill."

Now she was risking her fingers altogether. It didn't make sense.

"I don't want my students to know I'm sick," she explained. "They need to believe that this is a normal retirement. If I lose all of my hair, they'll know I'm ill, for sure. I can get by with the neuropathy; I don't play the piano that much during their lessons."

"I guess that makes sense," I said, even though it didn't. As a writer, I figured I'd be petrified by the idea of losing the use of my fingers. I thought it would be even scarier for my mother, who found comfort during the most difficult periods of her life by practicing Rachmaninoff for hours in our living room.

The first few rounds of chemo—which she had in Baltimore at Johns Hopkins—had us feeling cocky. My mom felt great after every treatment, and the steroids she received with her mix kept her wired. She rode her stationary bike for an hour every morning.

Meanwhile, Brette and I fell into a routine that called on all of our type A skills. Brette did most of the traveling to Maryland and kept my mom entertained during her long hours of infusion. She bought our mom's nurses fancy makeup. She told them cute stories about Ben.

I worked on getting recommendations for doctors in Boston for after her move.

My mom didn't have much disposable income as a piano teacher, but when she became a single parent at forty, she bought every kind of disability and long-term health insurance she could afford. We planned to use all of it now—every service, every bit of help we could get.

After just three treatments, Mom's tumor marker numbers dropped to the single digits. She was eating more than she ever had (she'd always been bad about remembering to have a meal in between piano lessons), so she looked healthier than before her diagnosis.

But by treatment six, the side effects began to kick in. Exhaustion took over for days at a time. She couldn't hold anything too hot or cold because extreme temperatures caused a stabbing pain in her fingers.

She came up to Boston often to prepare for her big move, and also to get a change of scenery and emotional support.

During one particular trip, just before she was finished teaching for good, I noticed a big problem. On our way home from the airport, I stared at her hair, which, on that day, looked like it had been dipped in cooking oil and left to dry.

"What's happening up there, Mom?" I asked, trying to keep my voice even.

"It's falling out," she said, her lower lip trembling. "I'm losing my hair."

"Well, they said that with this chemo, you'd still lose some—just not all," I reminded her.

"It's *all* falling out," she said in a whisper.

"It doesn't look like that to me. It just looks like you've stopped brushing and washing it."

"If it doesn't stop coming out, I'll be bald," she said, the tears now flowing.

From where I stood, she still had *a lot* of hair.

My mom's hair had always been big and curly, what I imagine Susan Sarandon's hair would look like if she stuck her finger in an electric socket. Even if some of it had fallen out, my mom still had more than your average human.

"I think we should wash and brush it," I told her. "I think that would make it look better."

"No," she said, her voice fragile. "I'm afraid to touch it."

I didn't know what to do.

Then I remembered something—an important piece of advice.

"I know where we can go," I said. "The Salon at 10 Newbury!"

A friend at work had told me about The Salon at 10 Newbury. After hearing about my mother's diagnosis, this friend—a *Globe* employee who'd been through cancer herself—advised that if we ever needed help with wigs and hair loss, it was the place to go in Boston.

"I'm taking you there," I told my mother before she could argue. "They'll know what to do."

"Okay," my mom said, looking doubtful.

Relief set in when I saw that The Salon at 10 Newbury didn't look like the wig shops we'd seen at the hospitals. I'd visited those departments with my mom in several medical facilities, and I could tell she felt doomed, so we left.

The Salon at 10 looked more like a place we'd visit by choice—like a splurge. It was fancy, and on one of the nicest stretches of retail in the Back Bay.

Patricia, the owner, found us within seconds. She was a soft-spoken woman, maybe in her sixties. She was petite like my mom; they kind of looked like sisters.

It must have been clear that my mom had spent the morning crying, because Patricia grabbed her hands and ushered us into a private room used for wig consultations. "Let's talk about it," she said.

My mom took a seat in the salon chair, her hands shaking, as Patricia asked questions.

Patricia could have had a career on NPR—her voice was steady and calm.

"Where are you in your cancer treatment?" she asked, as if we were talking about our plans for the weekend—like the word "treatment" wasn't a big deal.

When my mom answered, explaining that she had colorectal cancer that had metastasized, Patricia didn't flinch. Her face suggested she heard that kind of diagnosis every day. Then she looked at my mom's hair and shrugged.

"This," she said, "this we can work with."

I took a full breath, and my mom's shoulders relaxed.

"I love you, Patricia," I thought.

I decided that there should be a monument made for Patricia. Maybe an award in her name.

Slowly and carefully, she brushed my mom's hair, molding it into its old shape and fluffing it where it had fallen flat. Some of it fell out in chunks, which made my mom whimper, but Patricia's voice never faltered.

"This is going to look good," she said matter-of-factly, and then worked at it until it did.

At the end of the appointment, Patricia taught my mom how to wear a scarf to preserve the hair she still had, and gave her instructions on how often to wash it.

"You'll get through the rest of the school year with this hair," she said. "You'll look fine for your students."

My mom sighed, and I assumed it was because protecting her students was the goal. She worried about them all the time.

I was so relieved that I excused myself to go to the bathroom, where I cried alone, privately celebrating that we'd finally heard some good news—even if it was about hair.

Later, as we celebrated the day's victory at the Parish Cafe near the Public Garden, my mom presented me with a more complicated problem—one that revealed another reason she'd chosen the chemo that affected her fingers.

"If I keep losing my hair—if this cancer becomes something I have to keep treating forever—do you think I'll ever be able to date again?"

Suddenly, everything made sense. That was *another* reason she'd prioritized keeping even some of her hair. That's why she was willing to risk her ability to play the piano without pain.

Considering my day job, I should have known.

Whereas I'd spent most of my life as a single person, and often made it a full year at a time without any romantic prospects at all, my mom almost *always* had a boyfriend or, at the very least, suitors on the horizon. Men hit on her in restaurants and on planes. During one of her visits to Boston, I'd watched some guy in his fifties try to pick her up at a stoplight on Boylston Street.

My mom—like Brette—had always been natural with the opposite sex. Somehow she knew how to flirt and when to touch their arms, ever so lightly, with confidence. I'd always been jealous.

During our post-hair-appointment meal, she confessed that she didn't want to lose that part of herself—the part that was so dateable. She didn't want to entertain the possibility that the cancer might mean the end of romance.

"Of course you'll date again," I said, because it had never even occurred to me that she wouldn't. "Many people date with an illness. Think about Brette and her Crohn's disease. It never stopped her, even though she's spent months at a time dealing with stomach cramps and horrible joint pain. Somehow, she's always been able to meet guys."

"That's true," my mom said, hopeful.

I told my mom that dozens of people had written in to *Love Letters* with similar concerns.

Trailing the snoopers and cheaters, the workplace companions, the single people dealing with dating fatigue, and the liner-uppers (people who wanted to lock down a new significant other before breaking up with their current one), were another pack of advice seekers, the chronically ill who wanted to know how to navigate their love lives.

They were frustrated by all the talk of pledging sickness and health in an established relationship, because what if you were sick and you hadn't met anyone yet? That was a different challenge.

Commenters had great empathy for these letter writers and sometimes confessed that they were dealing with similar problems. They said the trick was to figure out how to see an illness as part of you, not all of you.

"Even with cancer?" my mom asked.

"I think so—because I have to believe my commenters," I told my mom. "Many of them have gone through this kind of thing, and many of them have found love."

My mom looked relieved, because she trusted my commenters, too. I was grateful that their virtual assurances meant as much as—or more than—mine did in real life.

"Let's go see *Iron Man 2*," I told my mom as we finished our sandwiches, and she lit up, because that sounded like a normal thing to do. All we wanted was normalcy, wherever we could find it.

On our way to the movie theater by Boston Common, I gave her a long look, because, at least in that moment, she looked like the mom I knew. Her hair was back to its wild and frizzy greatness, even if there was slightly less of it than there used to be.

"You look great," I told her, because it was true.

DATING WITH A CHRONIC ILLNESS

Q. I have been struggling with this situation for some time and I thought it might help if I gained some perspective.

I have been dealing with a very painful, chronic medical condition that has dominated my life for the past five years. Without going into the boring details I can tell you that this condition is not life threatening (for which I am very, very grateful) but does require occasional rounds of IV drug therapy. I also deal with moderate to severe pain on a daily basis, which can be difficult at times but I am much better at handling it than I used to be. To say that this illness has changed my life would be an understatement. It has virtually transformed my outlook on life to be more positive and open to change.

Despite these personal epiphanies, I find I have a blind spot in regards to the dating world. During the first two years of my illness I dated a close friend. It got fairly serious but we weren't meant to be (and it didn't end well). Aside from our other issues, I knew then that my illness put a lot of pressure on the relationship and it was very difficult for my partner to deal with it. This knowledge has become a roadblock during my various dating attempts since my last relationship. When I meet someone I am interested in, I feel very guilty and overwhelmed by the idea that my illness is too much of a burden to ask this nice, unsuspecting guy to take on. I also begin to worry about how and when to disclose this personal information. It is difficult for the subject to come up organically in conversation, aside from asking, "Have you heard any interesting medical stories lately? Well, I have this thing..." Usually, I become so stressed I immediately stop any attempt to pursue a relationship with said guy.

I know that I talk a big game about being positive and being open to change when deep down I am afraid. I have witnessed the impact of my health on the people I love and I want to spare others the pain of not being able to "fix" my situation. My illness is always going to be in the picture, and there is no simple "cure." My fear of becoming a burden leads me to choose to be alone and it makes me sad. How should I approach dating in regards to my health? Should I stop dating altogether? I would like to be able to share myself with someone despite all my health-related baggage.

—Suffering from Chronic Fear in California

A. Don't stop dating. And don't ever say, "Well, I have this thing." This doesn't have to be a solemn disclosure.

We're all difficult to date for one reason or another. Those who are always healthy might not appreciate life like you do. And maybe, unlike other people, you come to the table without mean parents, self-esteem issues, or a career that will take you away from your personal life. From where I sit, you're an emotionally present person who's self-sufficient despite your illness. You said it best: "*It has virtually transformed my outlook on life to be more positive and open to change.*" I mean, how many people can actually say that about themselves?

I don't want to make you roll your eyes by telling you that everything's peachy and that everyone is open to dating someone with a chronic illness, but I do think that many people would be into you. There are some truly miserable, healthy people out there who have rendered themselves undateable just because they have a bad attitude. You sound like a fantastic potential partner.

My advice? Reframe the importance of this illness in your own brain and then disclose it like you would anything else. As in, "I like hiking, biking, hanging out with my friends, and I'm strangely resilient because I've learned to deal with a chronic illness. You'll never catch me whining about little things." All of that's true, right?

I get this question a lot from people with illnesses—and, in a different way, from people who are recently divorced. They often assume that their bad experience is the first and only thing that prospective partners will notice about them. But I assure you that the rest of the world sees the entire package.

You're not asking anyone to "take you on." You're not looking to be someone's burden. You're asking nice people to hang out with you and date you. They should be so lucky.

—Meredith

READERS? WHAT DO YOU THINK?

Meredith is right, you need to re-prioritize your illness as part of your total "package." Don't let the disease define you. Sure, it will limit some activities but it's just a small part of the terrific package you want to present.
— THEREALJBAR

One thing you don't mention: Is the illness visible on early dates, something that needs clarification from the get-go? If not, wait a bit to see if your next potential guy is compatible before announcing it, like Mere suggested, without great fanfare and with pride in terms of how it has shaped your life for the better (e.g., out of pain there is growth and change and maturity for life challenges).
— OLDERNOWISER

I am currently battling cancer and, although I admit to sometimes feeling a little sorry for myself, realize how it has made me a more positive person overall. You have such a great outlook, so keep plugging away and just be the candid and positive person you are. — DAAL

Chapter 8

Man Up

As the column grew, so did the number of critics and trolls.

The *Globe* tried to stay ahead of abusive commenters and to protect readers, but it was increasingly difficult.

I let the moderators know that in most cases, criticism of me was okay. I'd set up the column so that people could disagree with my advice. I had thick skin.

Every now and then, though, it was difficult to maintain it. Sometimes I couldn't help but get defensive when I read some of the commenters' evaluation of my shortcomings.

The most vocal of my critics had one major accusation—that I was "sexist." They said I was too tough on male letter writers and that I let the women get away with selfish behavior. One reader rejected the entire column because of my great misandry.

"Why is it that the woman—no matter what she does—always gets sympathy in *Love Letters*?" the critic asked. "She can have an affair, pose naked, flirt compulsively—no matter what, typically she's made a 'mistake,' and rarely does she get criticized. Of course, for the men it's another story. They always have to shape up or mend their ways. This column is worthless because it is so biased."

I didn't believe this complaint had any merit.

First, when it came to my advice, I was pretty sure I was too easy on *everyone*. My softness was intentional; I wanted to write the kind of advice I'd give in real life, and in person, people don't respond well to tough love and judgmental directives. I figured the letter writers would get more from my feedback if I acted like a real friend, someone who'd empathize as much as possible and ask the right questions.

Second, when I did get assertive, it wasn't only with male letter writers. Readers sometimes assumed I was being tough on a man when the letter writer was, in reality, a woman. Most *Love Letters* entries were from straight, cisgender people, but that wasn't always the case.

In an early letter, for instance, a woman had written in because she was having trouble getting over her ex, who was also a woman. Commenters—who made assumptions based on pronouns—answered, "Man up!" They scolded the woman—whom they assumed was a straight man—for being overemotional, sensitive, and a wimp. I remember that someone called the letter writer a "Nancy boy." (I had to google "Nancy boy" to make sure I understood what they meant.)

Eventually, though, after one or two commenters floated the idea that the letter writer might be gay, some people decided to alter their advice. They retracted their "man up!" directives and offered more constructive ideas about how to cope with loss.

The collective pivot exposed that for many readers, it

wasn't appropriate for a man to be sad about a breakup, but women were allowed to feel miserable and dumped.

"I'm not the one with the bias," I thought to myself as I read their responses.

I tried to be aware of my limitations as a columnist, and to consider how being a straight white woman might inform my advice. But being hard on men, in general, was not something that kept me up at night.

My paternal grandfather, on the other hand, who read the column from the Golda Meir House, a senior living center near Boston, told me it might be something to think about. Grandpa Marty—who thought it was hilarious that someone as single as myself would be advising other people about their love lives—said he'd long believed that I was too critical of men, in general. He also argued that I didn't have enough empathy for people who wanted to have more "traditional experiences" when it came to heterosexual dating.

"Being a feminist doesn't mean you're not allowed to let someone do something nice for you," Grandpa Marty said. "You never let men pay. You always want things to be equal. You have to let men be men—let them be romantic."

I'd usually respond with an eye roll.

Grandpa Marty's only concerning accusation was that I sometimes spoke of men (straight men, to be specific) as if they were less capable—that they couldn't be trusted to understand a problem, show up for loved ones, or follow through.

He wondered if that's how I really felt, and if so, how my opinion affected my column.

I thought about this, and admitted that I did feel that way sometimes. The quality time I was spending in hospitals wasn't helping.

My mom was prepping for surgeries, which meant that Brette and I were toggling between medical offices, dealing with practicalities. Brette would spend hours on the phone each day waiting to speak with hospital receptionists and insurance reps. Her life had become hold music, and sometimes she used two phones at the same time, both on speaker. KT Tunstall vs. Michael Bublé. One Sara Bareilles song vs. another.

The best reps on the other end of the line were women, who always managed to answer our questions. We could tell they felt accountable.

Then, when it finally came time for my mom's operations, I noticed what I'd already seen in so many waiting rooms and chemo cubicles since the diagnosis: mothers, sisters, wives, and daughters, standing like security guards by hospital beds, working round the clock as advocates for their loved ones.

Not to mention the nurses, who were still mostly female.

Men were there, too—I knew this—but often, they seemed to have lighter tasks. I saw many of them dispatched by a family matriarch to get bagels. They made sure everyone had water.

Brette noticed this, too, and even saw it with Ben. Whenever he'd come to support the three of us at an appointment, he'd ask, "Anyone need water? Can I get you some water?"

It was as if there was some innate, male hunting and gathering thing happening, like he felt a driving force to make sure that the women in his pack weren't dehydrated.

Brette appreciated that Ben was around for our family during this stressful time, but she always thought he could do more. She wanted him to anticipate our needs, beyond beverages.

It also didn't help that my mom never mentioned the men from her past. Before a surgery one afternoon, I asked her whether she wished her most recent ex were still in her life so she could have his support and companionship during this difficult time.

She had been madly in love with that guy, at least until they stopped agreeing about their shared future and broke up. I'd always wondered whether they'd get back together.

My mom's response was, "No way. He wouldn't have wanted to be around cancer. He wouldn't be good at this kind of thing."

I knew this kind of statement was probably affecting me. I just didn't know how much.

Eventually, my bias was confirmed in real life. It happened the first time I met some of the commenters.

The regular readers had asked me, via email and in the comments section, to host a *Love Letters* party in Boston, so that at the very least, the New England–based crew could mingle.

The idea scared me. It was one thing to banter with Rico, BackBayBabe, and TheRealJBar online, but in person? What if they were confrontational? What if they had 7,000 cats or spoke like Gollum from *The Lord of the Rings*? It was all possible, but it seemed worth the risk. It was sort of like a blind date—probably a good idea as long as I was careful. I posted a note in the column saying that we'd all meet at Noir, a small bar at the Charles Hotel in Harvard Square. Hotel management told me that the venue could accommodate about 100 people.

My worst fear was that no one would show up.

Just in case people did show, though, I bought a stack of small name tags so that commenters could write down their screen handles and identify one another.

For a few minutes that night, the bar was empty, and I feared that maybe every single commenter had secretly been my mother and sister, logging in as different personalities to make me feel like someone was reading the column.

But then, out of nowhere, there was a line out the door. A crowd. Several hundred people trying to get into a small hotel bar. People used the name tags—some of them writing down their online nicknames—just as I'd hoped. Everyone was mingling and hugging each other like they were old friends, which I guess they sort of were.

It was surreal, walking around the room and seeing what the commenters looked like. It was also nice to know that the readership was diverse—that so many people who might never interact in real life had been gathering on the website every day.

To my great delight, the regular commenters were nothing like Gollum. TheRealJBar was a lovely woman whose real-life personality matched her no-nonsense advice. Sally and Alice were magnetic women who got along with each other as well in person as they did online. Valentino was a friendly wiseass. MHouston was a singer; she did an impromptu performance during the party.

Rico did not show up—or if he did, he didn't identify himself—but we all talked about what he might look like.

Part of me wanted to get closer to them—to ask for their real names and numbers, and to scream "What am I supposed to do when I'm lonely and freak out about my mom?"—but I maintained the boundary.

I figured I wasn't supposed to know everybody in real life, even though it was tempting.

I did have one big surprise that night, which gave me the reality check I needed.

One of my commenters from the start of the column was Two-Sheds, a thoughtful daily contributor whose advice was all about keeping calm. I imagined that Two-Sheds was in her fifties, perhaps someone who wore antique necklaces. In my fantasies, she looked like a younger Holland Taylor—or Angela Bassett.

At the party, I got the chance to meet Two-Sheds—and was forced to deal with an upsetting reality.

"I'm Two-Sheds," Two-Sheds said, after approaching me with his wife.

"You can't be Two-Sheds," I said, looking at the thirty-something bespectacled blondish man in front of me. "You're a man."

"I'm Two-Sheds," Two-Sheds repeated. "And I am a man."

"But you can't be a man," I said, stunned. "Because… Two-Sheds…she's…. so…thoughtful."

There it was.

I thanked Two-Sheds for his participation and later left the party knowing that I also made too many assumptions, just like the commenters. Sometimes I was right, but not always.

I vowed to do better. At least I'd try.

I WANT TO SWEEP A LADY OFF HER FEET

Q. I'm a twenty-five-year-old attorney who graduated from law school last year and I hope to get into politics someday. Aside from my career aspirations, I am desperately looking for a girl I can sweep off her feet.

I have never had a problem finding pretty girls and have always been a sucker for intellectuals like myself. But what I have found repeatedly is that I always run into two types of women. There's the feminist types who hate being treated like a lady (hold doors, pay for dinner, walk on the outside of the curb, etc.) and put their careers before anything or anyone else. Then there are the girls who use me because I have a good career and are only interested in what I can do for them (concerts, purses, jewelry, all within three weeks of the relationship), but never get emotionally attached.

I have always called myself a hopeless romantic because I believe that all the money in the world is only as good as the one you can share it with. More or less, I want to love and be loved. I want to take a walk, look at the stars, and get lost in the moment. I want to make a girl a romantic dinner and go out for ice cream. A girl who I can bring lunch to at work just because it's a Tuesday. A girl who likes it when little notes are left in her car and apartment—just to brighten her day. Meredith, I don't consider myself clingy (forty hours workweek-plus as an attorney); I am just someone who is looking for the real deal and not just a facade of love. You know? Where are these girls, the ones who want to truly love and be loved? The ones who measure life not in minutes, money, or promotions but in moments? Is it that in the politically correct world we live in today there is finally no room for a hopeless romantic?

—Lost Without Love, Boston

A. I blame romantic comedies for making people think they're supposed to sweep someone (or be swept) off their feet for no good reason. I'm all for feet-sweeping, but that should be the second or third step in any good relationship. The first step is getting to know someone as a peer.

My guess is that the women who aren't letting you pay for their dinners (the dreaded feminists!) are put off by your approach. Your immediate push for romance seems disingenuous—and I'm pretty sure it is. My advice: When you meet a woman, really talk to her. No lines. No notes. Just real talk. Then, if you really like her—and respect her—you can take her for ice cream or whatever it is you want to do. Romance means so much more when you actually know the person you're dating. It doesn't sound like you get far enough with these women to know whether there's any real connection.

Whatever you do, cut it out with the anti-feminist talk. It's ridiculous. You say you want to find a woman who wants to be treated like a lady, but most women want to be treated like a human. Think about how you'd want to be treated, so behave accordingly. Be a friend.

Perhaps dating a fellow lawyer would work. Your salary and time spent at work would probably be equal. You'd be able to see through each other's posturing. You'd have something real in common. Just a thought.

—Meredith

READERS? WHAT DO YOU THINK?

Gee, I thought Meredith was kind of rough on this guy… — AWS34

You know what the most romantic thing you can do for a woman is? Listen to her. Amazingly, it will also help you follow Meredith's excellent advice of getting to know her better. We do often want to get swept off our feet, etc., but we want it to be for the right reasons—because the guy loves us for who we are, as unique individuals, and not because we are the most willing prop for his romantic hero fantasy. At thirty-five, you will be expected to pay for dinner. At twenty-five, when the women you are dating are just getting their footing as independent adults and take rightful pride in their ability to support themselves, it's threatening and can feel dismissive of the identity they are working so hard to build. — KRAKEN77

I'm a feminist and I love it when men hold doors and, especially, walk on the outside of the curb (a remnant from the time streets were muddy and men were protecting women from having their hoop skirts splashed). But Meredith is dead on—this letter writer is not looking for a real relationship with a real human being, but some kind of romantic fantasy into which he can plug a pretty little doll. He means well, I'm sure. But he has A LOT of growing up to do. — READERGIRL23

HE SHOULD HAVE CALLED ME AN UBER

Q. I met "Jack" online and we've been seeing each other for about one month. I like him very much. We are both in our thirties and live in the city. All signs point to us having real relationship potential. We've been out several times, met some of each other's friends, text each other every day, and occasionally talk on the phone to catch up. We both took down our profiles. Last weekend he slept over at my place. It was nice.

Here's what has me questioning whether I should ever see him again: Last night he had me over to his place for a home-cooked dinner and Netflix. Dinner was delicious and he did all the dishes—so romantic. We cuddled up together on the couch for a movie and he gave me a massage. Perfect date so far! Before the end of the movie, we go to his bedroom. That was great.

Then, as we are lying in each other's arms, he starts yawning and talking about how early he needs to get up for work the next day and how he is sure I also need to wake up early…and basically suggests that I should go home! He didn't even walk me to the front door of his building. At 10:30 p.m., I had to walk three blocks to the train to get home.

I felt so stung. The next morning I still feel awful. He keeps texting me as usual, thanking me for a "great time" last night (which sounds so crass now) and telling me about his morning at work. If he knew he didn't want me to stay over last night, I wish he had made that clear before I came over. Or had not hooked up with me. Or had at least been more considerate about the exit—he could have called me an Uber and walked me to the sidewalk.

So, finally, my question: Do I confront him in the hopes that this was some clueless oversight or do I block his number and give him the fade because he is clearly a cad and he made me feel cheap? Ever since I left his place I have been barely resisting the latter option. Please advise!

—Kicked Out

A. He gets a pass on this one—for now. Not everyone assumes that sleepovers are cool on weeknights in the beginning of a relationship. And depending on where he lives, he might not have thought much of a walk to the train at 10:30 p.m.

Yes, he should have escorted you to the front door (I bet you would have walked him to your front door or called him a car had he been at your place), but let's give him the benefit of the doubt.

See him again and communicate. Let him know that you're not into bedroom stuff if it means having to throw on clothes and run to the train fifteen minutes later. Tell him that you'd rather be able to sleep over and relax.

Also do the mirroring thing. When he leaves your house late at night, offer to get him an Uber. Bring the chivalry and set an example.

It was a weird night, but not everybody gets it right in the beginning.

—Meredith

READERS? WHAT DO YOU THINK?

Call your own Uber. — CHICKEN LITTLE

Why should she? Why shouldn't he be a gentleman? — REINDEERGIRL

Well, ReindeerGirl, I hope the men in your world are complete gentlemen and treat you like a princess. And that's all I'm gonna say about that. — CHICKEN LITTLE

Jeez, the only thing he didn't do is leave money on the night table. — MOVA

Chapter 9

Cursed

I can't tell you how many times I've told letter writers to go to therapy. Hundreds of times. Almost every time.

Sometimes it seemed silly to write an advice column if all I was going to do was tell people to go talk to someone else, but I thought of the referral process as my duty. Letter writers emailed me privately to tell me they were raised in repressed New England homes where it was shameful to discuss your problems with an outsider. Others told me they didn't even know how to find a therapist. "How do I know whether my insurance covers it? How do I find the right one for me?" they'd ask, and then we'd email until we figured out a plan.

I lived my own advice. By the time I'd started *Love Letters*, I'd been in therapy on and off (but mostly on) for almost twenty years. During that time, I'd seen a handful of therapists and psychologists, but two became long-term advisors who shaped how I managed my own relationships.

The first was Dr. Song, whose office was down the street

from the mall in Columbia, Maryland. My mom brought me to Dr. Song when I was a teenager because she wanted me to talk about how I was affected by the divorce. She worried that my disintegrating relationship with my father would affect how I dealt with men, in general. The only men I seemed to enjoy were the famous and fictional ones whose pictures were taped up around our house.

I think my mom also brought me to therapy because she thought I might be gay and closeted. I suspected this because Dr. Song often wanted me to talk about one of my best friends in high school, Elizabeth, who'd told me she was attracted to women.

"I want you to know, Meredith," Dr. Song would say, as she pushed her Sally Jessy Raphael glasses up her nose, "that it doesn't matter if you'd decide you're attracted to women, too. Frankly, I don't care if you come in one day and tell me you're attracted to a tomato plant."

"You should probably be concerned if I tell you I'm attracted to a tomato plant," I thought.

Dr. Song said the line about the tomato plant so many times that to this day, whenever I pass a fresh produce market, I expect something meaningful to happen.

My relationship with Dr. Song had long-lasting effects because she spoke to me like a peer—like I wasn't a patient. Sometimes we'd use our billable hour to walk over to the Wawa convenience store near her office, and she'd buy me a Diet Coke.

"I just need a break from all of these appointments," she'd tell me in her "Calgon, take me away" voice, which made me feel like an adult woman friend she'd met for a cocktail after work.

It was a good trick; we talked about everything on those walks—including my parents' divorce—and it felt like collaboration, like I knew as much as she did.

The only problem was that the trick worked too well. I was given the false impression that I was my therapist's peer, and that instead of her helping me process my problems, I was doing it myself and letting her tag along for the ride.

This issue became clear years later, in my mid-twenties, when I found my second long-term therapist, Dr. Thomas.

I had taken a short break from counseling, but it felt like time to return. My friends were dating with ease, and I couldn't figure out how to join them. They seemed capable of liking more people than I did. I was also still getting over my college boyfriend and couldn't figure out why it was taking so long to let go.

I called a friend who was getting her PhD in psychology at Suffolk University and asked her to recommend a good professional. For some reason I can't remember, I asked if she knew any good therapists who were men. I think I wanted to see if the experience would be different.

"I'll give you information for Dr. Thomas," my friend said. "He's on the list of recommended psychologists in the area. Looks like he specializes in eating disorders."

"But I don't have an eating disorder," I told her.

"Yeah, but that's not all he does, and it probably means he's used to dealing with women," she said.

There was a catch with Dr. Thomas; his office was in Salem, Massachusetts, which was about forty-five minutes from my apartment at the time. But it seemed worth it; mental health came first.

The location, though, made it difficult for me to take our appointments seriously.

Downtown Salem is a legitimate theme park of witchery, where almost every storefront advertised psychic readings, T-shirts with broomsticks, and ingredients for spells and curses. It was a challenge to focus on self-actualization after seeing so many crystal balls on the way to appointments.

The city made me feel a bit cursed, really. I'd spend my hour with Dr. Thomas talking about bad experiences at home or work, and then walk out of his office to see hexes and voodoo dolls everywhere.

One day I found myself browsing a local shop for love spells for Patrick. What if they worked?

Another distraction was the board game.

Under Dr. Thomas's desk was a board game called The Dinosaur's Journey to High Self-Esteem. Based on the colorful box, which showed tiny dinosaurs wearing human clothing, I assumed the game was like Candy Land, but with feelings instead of treats. Sometimes when I was supposed to be talking about why I wasn't dating or, years later, how I felt about my mom being sick, I found myself distracted by the poor dinosaurs in their overalls and dresses, and wondered why they needed so much validation.

"Have you ever played it?" I asked Dr. Thomas once, pointing to the board game, when I knew he was trying to have an important conversation.

"Yes," he said, his mustache twitching. "I have."

Dr. Thomas and I had many silent struggles for power. He claimed that I came to my appointments "pre-processed," that

I'd already talked everything through with myself and decided, before arriving, what everything meant.

I admitted that my day job made it difficult to stop myself from coming to quick conclusions about my feelings.

"Try not to define it first," he told me. "Try to *feel* it. Tell me everything you feel about what's going on with your mom, especially now that she's moved to Boston. How has her proximity changed your life?"

I didn't want to talk about that.

The good news when it came to my mom was that two big surgeries were over. Her colorectal tumor had been removed, as well as a few of the lung metastases. After recuperating and moving to Boston, she would do more chemotherapy at Mass General, and then doctors would consider another surgery for the remaining metastases in her lungs.

She was happy in Boston and loved the city. She'd found an apartment in a former piano factory in the South End, which meant there was enough room in the building's elevator to move in her Steinway grand. She liked her new doctors and had a cool nurse named John.

But her new home was 1.5 miles from my condo, which meant that I was always on call.

"You're living this even more now," Dr. Thomas said. "There will be less time for yourself. Boundaries with your mother will be harder to maintain. We still do a lot of talking about you missing Patrick, but is that who's really on your mind?"

"Yes," I told Dr. Thomas, frustrated. "I still miss Patrick. Like, all the time.

"Anyway," I continued, "my mom is like my best friend. I *love* hanging out with her."

"I imagine it's more complicated than that," he said, provoking one of my "I'm not going to talk about this" shrugs.

It was a constant struggle because I liked being the boss of feelings and telling other people what to do with them. Sometimes my sessions with Dr. Thomas felt like thumb-wrestling.

He also told me, during a particularly frustrating session, that I was, quite literally, sitting in his chair.

"You're sitting in *my chair*. You've been sitting in the wrong place for years," he said, pointing to where I reclined in a brown fabric piece of furniture.

"What do you mean '*your* chair'?" I asked, clutching the arms of the seat that supported me through an hour of therapy every week.

Dr. Thomas scowled.

"You walked in on that first day and sat down in that chair, but it's *my* chair. All of my other patients sit on the *couch*. Patients usually sit on the couch, right? They lie down on the couch."

I could tell he'd wanted to say this for years. I wondered why he hadn't.

Dr. Thomas needed to learn to be more assertive, I concluded. That's what I'd tell him if he wrote me a letter.

"Do you want me to move to the couch now?" I asked.

"Too late now," he said, shaking his head.

Dr. Thomas suspected that I gravitated to the chair because I saw it as the seat of power. I swore I chose it because it looked softer and more comfortable than the couch, but deep down, I wasn't sure.

The chair *was* the position of authority in the room. I didn't want to move to the couch.

Despite all the many ways I tried to stop Dr. Thomas from forcing me to face how I really felt about the scary things in my life, he did manage to push me forward, at least when it came to my breakup.

On a random summer weeknight, I arrived at therapy and took my regular seat—in Dr. Thomas's chair. I was miserable about Patrick again. He and I had resumed communication—we were starting to exchange some nice texts about office gossip, and it felt good. But then I heard from a mutual friend that he was seeing someone.

I admitted to myself that I felt betrayed—and stupid—because I thought Patrick and I had the same thing on our minds. I assumed it was clear to both of us that we missed each other and were finding our way back to coupledom.

But he was with someone else, and this mutual friend told me Patrick had *traveled* with this woman—for a whole romantic weekend. We'd never made time for that.

I was lonely and wanted to talk about it. I wanted to wallow in it with Dr. Thomas.

But before I could tell him the news—and declare, as I sometimes did, that I would never date again—I noticed he looked nervous. He avoided making eye contact.

"There's something I have to tell you," Dr. Thomas said.

I was worried because that kind of sentence sounded a lot like "we need to talk." Or "let me show you this scan."

"Just tell me," I said, my voice flat. "Oh God, just tell me."

"I met Patrick," Dr. Thomas said.

"What?"

"I *met Patrick*," he repeated. "I haven't been able to figure out whether I should tell you, but I think I should."

I took a deep breath and fell back into my favorite brown seat, as he leaned forward on the patient's couch.

Dr. Thomas explained that he'd attended a social event that forced him into a casual conversation with a man named Patrick. Based on how this Patrick looked and what he did for a living, Dr. Thomas knew he was *the* Patrick, the guy he'd been hearing about for years now, before and after the relationship.

"I'll confess to extending the conversation," Dr. Thomas said. "I asked him a few questions so I could hear him talk—I wanted to keep talking to him—because... it was Patrick!"

"You got Patrick in 3-D—the IMAX experience," I said, feeling like the therapist, trying to help him through it. "It must have been strange for you."

"Right!" Dr. Thomas said. "It *was* strange."

I understood why he looked so pleased yet confused. It was sort of like when I'd met my letter writers and commenters. Crossing the line into real life was as disorienting as it was exciting. You had to reset your brain.

I asked, "So? Was Patrick all you thought he'd be and more?"

I waited for Dr. Thomas to tell me that Patrick and I were clearly opposites and that our breakup was for the best. I waited for him to tell me that Patrick was too old for me, because Dr. Thomas had always suspected I'd wind up with a younger man.

"Well," he said, "you didn't tell me he was so good-looking. He's very attractive, Meredith. I didn't realize that."

"What?" I barely got the word out because of the painful tightness in my chest.

"I said he's very good-looking," he repeated.

I'd never had transference, never experienced romantic feelings for Dr. Thomas, but in that moment I was jealous of Patrick. I wanted Dr. Thomas to think *I* was good-looking. I wanted him to think I was the better catch.

Dr. Thomas, who'd been so good at reading me for so many years, didn't seem to understand my facial expressions in the moment—because he kept talking.

"Based on what you told me, I had pictured an average-looking guy. But he's *very good-looking*."

"Okay," I said. "I get it... I mean... are you trying to say he's way better-looking than I am? That you're surprised we dated because he's *that* hot?"

"No... I mean... no."

Dr. Thomas shriveled on the couch as he realized where he'd led me.

"He's just better-looking than I expected," he said, careful and slow with his words.

"Okay," I mumbled, jumping to the conclusion that people thought Patrick and I were mismatched not because we had different interests but because he was apparently so attractive that Dr. Thomas wanted to take his pants off.

Reading my body language, Dr. Thomas changed the subject, asking me about my mother and Brette, clearly hoping I would stop spiraling. I pretended I had moved on from the conversation, smiling and talking about the latest news from the hospital.

I did not tell Dr. Thomas that he had set me in motion. For the first time, I thought about finding a boyfriend who wasn't Patrick. Like, soon.

And I wanted that person to be so hot that when Dr.

Thomas accidentally ran into him at a social event, he would forget Patrick ever existed.

I sat in my therapist's chair and began to strategize about how to make my next move. That was what Dr. Thomas probably wanted anyway.

SCARED TO SEE HIS THERAPIST

Q. I have been in a solid, loving relationship for the past seven months. We fell for each other hard and fast.

Here's the tricky part. He was depressed for much of his younger years and has found solace in going to therapy. As our relationship has gotten more and more serious, he is urging me to attend these sessions with him.

My question is this: Should I be worried that a relationship should need therapy after such a short time or should I be thankful that my boyfriend values our relationship and wants me to be a part of this area of his life? Thanks for the advice!

—Therapy Scares the Bejesus Out of Me, Boston

A. Don't be scared. He doesn't want to bring you to therapy because he thinks that you're a mess as a couple. He's bringing you because therapy is a big part of his life and because he wants you to understand what's going on in his noggin.

Go at least once. It'll either be okay—maybe even enlightening and helpful—or it'll reveal something bad that you needed to know anyway. You don't have to commit to more than one session. You can ask the therapist once you're there whether this is something that you need to be a part of on a regular basis.

My guess is that your boyfriend just wants to put your relationship through his system of checks and balances. Nice that he wants you to be a part of something that makes his life better.

—Meredith

READERS? WHAT DO YOU THINK?

If he needs constant therapy, time for you to move on. Plenty of folks out there that need no more therapy than a night out with the boys or falling asleep in your arms. If that is not enough for them then NEXT! — JUPITER03

Therapy is this guy's religion. No harm in attending a service. If he starts pushing you to convert then you can reassess. — PATRICIAFD

I'm a therapist myself, and I don't think you have anything to worry about. My guess is that this is just a really important part of his life, and he wants to let you in on it. — WHYNOT13

Maybe I am a complete voyeur, but it kind of sounds like fun. — BATESIE52

Chapter 10

The Nucleus

I knew that getting dates would be a complicated and possibly time-consuming task, mainly because my inbox was full of letters from fatigued singles who wondered what they were doing wrong. They asked whether I knew some secret to finding a mate. I did not.

I wondered how Patrick had met the woman he was dating, and guessed that he'd seen her at a Holy Cross sporting event. She was probably all decked out in his favorite team's gear, looking all cute and open to having children.

I'd never known how to advise readers who'd hit a wall with dating, because there was no magic way to strategize the procurement of a partner, despite what so many self-help books would have them believe.

Sometimes, in my answers to frustrated single letter writers, I'd write unhelpful things like "Maybe you should join a sports team!" or "Take a class!" which, for the record, was terrible advice, because the few classes I'd taken at the Boston

Center for Adult Education in my twenties were packed with straight single women, who were clearly expecting more men to sign up for "Intro to Guitar."

The quickest way for letter writers to meet people was to date online, so I often advised them to sign up for a new app or site. But I didn't want to go that route myself. Four years into the column, I'd answered hundreds of questions about various dating apps and websites, but I'd never been on an online date.

Part of it was laziness, but it was also fear. The process seemed to involve a lot of rejection, and, every so often, lies.

Another reason I stayed offline was that I wanted to preserve my privacy, which was disappearing as the column became more popular. It's not that I thought I was getting famous, or even "Boston famous," like my friend Jenny, who hosted a local food show and often got recognized at restaurants.

The only place I'd ever been recognized was at a bowling alley in Dorchester. "That's Meredith Goldstein from *Love Letters*," a coworker had heard the person in the lane next to us say. I'm sure it helped that I'd entered my name as "Meredith G." on the screen above the lanes.

I still count that night as one of the most exciting of my life.

But there were new, less friendly people in the comments section, and more critics on other websites who sometimes said mean things about my face and body. Whenever I thought about making a dating profile, I imagined it screen-grabbed and tweeted. Even if I was just being paranoid, I knew I should stay offline.

I also didn't want readers to think I was endorsing a specific dating website. Letter writers often asked whether I recommended one site over another, so choosing Match.com over

PlentyofFish.com for myself felt like a conflict of interest. I didn't want to have to lie.

But dating without websites left few options. Basically, none.

I began to long for an imaginary person I hadn't thought about in years. We called him: The Nucleus.

In my twenties, when I was still living with Jess, we often sat around with our friend Danielle and talked about dating experiences. Both Jess and Danielle had survived a string of terrible online dates. One man left Jess an irate voicemail after she rejected him, telling her he was better off without her because she "sounded like a man." Another man asked her about her hobbies during their first date. She mentioned that she liked all things design and travel, and he responded by telling her he liked the outdoors—and to "back into things."

"Back into things?"

"Yes, back into things," he said, giving her a confident smile.

"I don't know what you mean. Like back into things with your car?"

"No, like... backing into a table. Or a dildo."

"Oh," Jess said.

Later I would tell her that this man should get credit for disclosing his sexual interests—good for him for knowing what he likes!—but Jess said it was too early for that kind of talk. She had no interest in seeing that particular man back into anything, ever.

When Jess and Danielle did go out with someone they liked, it was just as bad. They had to accept the reality that those men might be scrolling through thousands of other faces. Jess and Danielle found themselves compulsively checking to see whether their dates had gone back online.

There were too many options for everyone, and they felt lost in the process.

Danielle, who was the most Malcolm Gladwellian of the three of us, had a theory about how we could all meet partners, perhaps all at the same time. She said we lacked one necessary thing, "The Nucleus."

"You see," Danielle said one night, plates of shrimp tempura rolls in our laps, the television on, "what we need is a nucleus. All we have to do is meet one guy—just one nice guy—who knows a bunch of *other* nice guys. His job is to connect us to his world. The nucleus doesn't even have to be single. Or a man. The person just has to be available to us, and then we can date his friends."

"Yes," Jess said, between sushi burps. "*That's* why we're single. We haven't had a nucleus."

We considered whether we'd been overlooking a possible nucleus in our friend group.

Paul, a friend from college whom I'd set up with my work friend Jenn, looked like a good nucleus, but he was a high school teacher, and ninety-nine percent of his coworkers were women also in need of a nucleus. Our close friend Brad, a nurse, was often surrounded by great people, but his friends were mostly gay men or straight women who reminded us of ourselves. My friend Pete from college couldn't be the nucleus because he was a sportswriter and he traveled too much. Mark only knew married dads.

Jess, Danielle, and I began to list our wishes for the nucleus as if we were Jane and Michael Banks summoning Mary Poppins.

"Maybe the nucleus works in tech," Danielle said.

"Yes. He works with computers," Jess agreed.

"The nucleus has great parties. He plans weekend trips with his friends," I offered.

"He's hilarious," Jess added.

"He likes to watch television," I said.

The nucleus was an important and wonderful person.

He was also imaginary because we never found him.

Jess and Danielle both met their partners online. I liked their spouses, but they couldn't connect me to other guys; they were also not the nucleus.

That left work, and finding another work romance seemed impossible. The changing media landscape meant that the *Globe* was further reducing its staff and doing more with less. Downsizing an office also means downsizing work romances.

With that in mind, I hinted to friends that I would consider going on blind dates if they knew anyone. I vowed that I would be open-minded. No sabotage.

One work friend knew a guy who was around my age and, like me, was interested in meeting someone in their thirties who didn't want to have children.

"Perfect!" I said, and tried to feel as enthusiastic as I sounded.

Before the date, I got a blowout. I wore a navy dress that I thought made my waist look nice.

I arrived at the restaurant early, so I decided to hit the bathroom before my date arrived. I figured I'd check my hair and pee.

Minutes later, when I was through with my toilet business, I went to wash my hands, but the soap dispenser was empty. I rummaged through my purse for hand sanitizer but didn't have any. I muttered a few expletives as I tried not to touch anything.

I walked out to the dining area to tell someone I needed soap, but before I could find an employee, my date—a smiling blond man who sort of looked like he could be Patrick's cousin—had arrived at the restaurant and was standing in front of me, reaching out to shake my hand. The same hand that I had not washed after relieving myself in the bathroom.

He took my hand and shook it. I winced and tried to remind myself that urine and feces are on everything and that it probably wasn't a big deal.

But it was gross. Especially when we ordered a hummus and pita plate to share, because they were finger foods, and I couldn't stop thinking about germs.

I thought about excusing myself to go back to the bathroom again to check for a soap refill, but that seemed like an odd move because he'd just seen me come out of the bathroom. Maybe someone used to first dates would have figured out a quick solution (or carried hand sanitizer for such an emergency)—or would have just forgotten about it—but I couldn't.

My date seemed very smart and said a lot of interesting things about his family. I hoped we could have a second date so I could concentrate. His post-date report to our mutual friend was that he thought it went well, but that when we left, I had given him an "awkward hug."

"But I'm a bad hugger!" I told our mutual friend. "And there could have been urine on my hands!"

My friend passed on the message that I'd had a good time. The guy did email, and we scheduled a second date, but he canceled before it happened. He told me he had seen an ex and that they'd decided to get back together.

I couldn't even be that upset because it was just one date.

The problematic thing was that I didn't know if I'd ever get set up again. Finding a single guy through a friend seemed to be a rare thing.

Part of me was relieved that I was quickly running out of options. That one date had made me really tired. When I wasn't thinking about washing my hands, I was thinking about my mom.

It was around this time that I learned, via the column and Facebook, that two of my most active readers, who'd long liked each other's one-liners in the comments section, had started dating after meeting at a *Love Letters* event I'd thrown after that first party.

Another one of the original commenters, Sally, was also in a new relationship that she could trace back to the column. She told me she'd planned a trip with her longtime *Love Letters* buddy, Alice, who'd become her friend in real life.

Alice wound up having to bail from the vacation at the last minute, but Sally decided she'd go alone. While away, she met a very attractive man at a bar. They were now dating long-distance, and she had plans to move to be with him.

This astounded me, that a comments section—a place often associated with trolls and malcontents—could also be a home where people shared the best of themselves. I never thought it could become a place where people could connect in real life.

I was happy for my commenters and amused by my passive role in the couplings. And then it hit me: For so long, my friends and I had been searching for that magic nucleus.

"Great," I said, picking up the phone to call Danielle with the news. "Guess what I am."

IS ONLINE DATING REQUIRED?

Q. I'm thirty-two years old and single. I love my job and my friends and am generally happy, but I would like to be in a relationship. My job is not conducive to meeting new people, and when I go out, I usually just want to spend time with my friends.

I recognize that online dating seems like the obvious way to meet people I wouldn't normally encounter, but I'm just not sure it's going to work for me. I hate the "u r so cute" messages from people who clearly aren't right for me; even nice messages from nice guys make me cringe at the thought of having to engage in back-and-forth banter with someone I don't know via email so that eventually we can meet up.

When that date is scheduled, I can't help thinking that I'd rather be spending time with friends, reading a book, or going to the gym. The post-date report always goes something like, "He was nice. It was fine." When asked if I want to see him again, the inevitable answer is, "I don't really care." I have met some truly decent guys, but I just can't seem to make myself care about someone I meet once or twice in such a forced situation.

I find small talk exhausting, and it takes me a while to feel comfortable around new people. When I have been excited about guys in the past, it is always someone I got to know before even considering him as a romantic partner, not someone I felt I had to evaluate after each meeting to decide if I want to see them again. My question, therefore, is if you think online dating can work for everyone.

Is it something I really should do, just to keep an open mind? Or is it legitimate to say, "This just isn't for me. Either I'll find someone in a more organic way, or I won't find someone at all"? I don't want to feel like I'm giving up (then regret it later), but it's just not clear to me that there will be any sort of payoff. Do you believe that some personalities are not compatible with online dating, or that I just need to try to adopt a more positive attitude and see what happens?

—An Introvert with a Dilemma, Central Mass.

A. Online dating isn't for everyone. You don't have to do it.

But you do have to change your attitude about first dates. My concern is that the problems you have with online dating sort of apply to all types of dating. Blind dates set up by friends aren't much more organic. If you meet someone at a party, you have to decide pretty quickly whether you want to see them again. You won't always have the luxury of getting to know someone before you fall for them. You have to learn how to connect with someone without months of bonding.

My advice is to do one thing a week to take you out of the gym, friends, and books. That thing could be browsing an online dating site and messaging one person. That thing could be going to a social event and talking to one person you don't know. You don't have to walk away with a phone number or plans for a date. It's just about changing your scenery and learning how to mingle without resenting the experience.

I don't expect you to become a different person or to develop a better attitude about guys who tell you that "u r so cute." I just want you to feel better about looking—and to carc enough to make the effort to get to know someone new.

—Meredith

READERS? WHAT DO YOU THINK?

I almost could have written this letter...I do think you could reevaluate your attitude toward first dates; if you are really that ambivalent (to put it mildly), then I don't know why you are even going on those first dates at all. Either find someone you have at least a modicum of excitement about meeting, or take a pass. — GALWAYGIRL

You do realize some level of engaging with men will be necessary, right? — HSMBS

Make some variation of this letter part of your online profile and that should pretty much take care of all of those interactions you want to avoid. — SUNALSORISES

HIS PROFILE IS ACTIVE

Q. I have been dating a guy I met on online for about a month and a half now. We have gone out about eight times or so. We hit it off right away and he was always the one to plan the next date and ask when he can see me again. One evening, we started talking about whether we're dating other people. He said he wasn't dating anyone else and didn't plan on it either, that he liked me a lot and wanted to see where things would go. We even discussed going away for the weekend in a few weeks.

I still have an active subscription to the dating website, even though I blocked my account so I wasn't "active." I know I shouldn't have done it, but out of curiosity, I went onto the dating website and checked out his profile. It shows that he has been active on the site, fairly frequently actually.

I know we haven't been seeing each other very long, but I guess I don't like to think I am developing feelings for someone only to be let down.

Am I wasting my time with this? Am I a filler while he continues to shop for the next best thing? What is the "protocol" with all of this online dating stuff?!

—To Date or Not to Date, NH

A. I can't read his mind or pretend to understand his intentions, but I wouldn't jump to any conclusions about the website. Maybe he logged in because he was bored. Maybe he was on the site to see what you had done with your profile.

Honestly, if you had met this guy through friends or at a bar, you'd have no idea how he represents himself when you're not there. You need to focus on how you feel when you're with him and whether the relationship seems to be growing.

If things continue to go well and you're at the point where you've stopped counting dates, feel free to ask him what he's done with his profile. Online daters almost always have to have this chat. It's awkward, but it's inevitable. There's no protocol; you just ask.

For the record, I don't think that you're a "filler." You're just in a new relationship. You're both figuring out whether you actually want each other. Online or offline, there are no guarantees.

—Meredith

READERS? WHAT DO YOU THINK?

Slow down. You're looking for signs of a commitment that he hasn't made yet. He seems to be interested so far. Remember that panic is never attractive. — WIZEN

Honestly, I would wait a few more dates later, and then ask him what's up. When I met my boyfriend (whom I now live with) online, he was ecstatic about canceling his membership and dedicating himself to our relationship. — RACHELIZ1818

Set up a bogus account, contact him via the dating website, and see how he responds. Then you'll have your answer. — MAKENOEXCUSES

Chapter 11

Draco

Many readers felt pressure to be friends with their exes.

One letter writer told us that when she explained to her ex that a friendship would hurt too much, he accused her of being closed-minded.

"He says it's unprogressive of me, someone who prides herself on being a liberal-minded person," she wrote. "Am I wrong to not try to just be his friend? Can lovers really be friends after such intimacy?"

Unprogressive. That was a new one.

I told letter writers that there was no obligation to be friends with an ex. That's one of the reasons breakups are supposed to require so much thought on the part of the dumpers. When you tell someone you're done, there are no assurances you'll get to keep them around in some other form. You have to be ready to say goodbye forever.

I did tell readers that if friendship felt right, it was worth a try.

Certain romantic relationships were mostly about the platonic stuff to begin with. In other cases, time healed wounds, and it was possible to start something new.

I hoped I could have a friendship with Patrick at some point. It was starting to seem possible, because as more months passed, I didn't fantasize as much about sharing anything romantic with him. I longed to talk to him about inconsequential things, like whether he was watching *Game of Thrones*. I wanted to gossip with him about our coworkers.

My favorite conversations with Patrick had always been about stuff he'd done when I wasn't around. I could listen to him talk about his job all day. I even liked listening to him talk about sports. He could be funny about anything.

In the office, my behavior toward Patrick was erratic. Sometimes I'd send him emails and he'd respond, thrilled that I seemed open to platonic discussion. Other times, when I saw him in person, I would avert my eyes and walk away.

Mark was also confused about our status.

"Are you talking to Patrick?" he'd ask.

"I don't know," I'd admit.

Patrick and I did follow some unspoken rules when we communicated. The big one was that we didn't mention our romantic lives. I knew through coworkers that he had another new girlfriend, but he never hinted that there was someone else around.

"Do you *need* this friendship?" Dr. Thomas asked. "Do you want to go down that 'friends' road again?"

The road he referred to was the one I went down with my college ex, the one I referred to in *Love Letters* as Draco Malfoy. Draco and I had tried to be friends. For years.

"I won't do that again," I promised.

Draco and I had a significant relationship in the context of college, but in reality we were together for less than a year.

After we broke up, though, we spent several years festering in what he called a friendship. That friendship involved us calling each other too much—almost daily or more. We lived in different cities after graduation, but visited each other like we were in a long-distance relationship. And when we stayed at each other's apartments, we often slept in the same bed, under the same blanket.

There was no kissing, but there was often almost-kissing. I'd still tuck my head into his armpit. Sometimes he'd put his lips on my forehead after saying good night.

Every time I saw him, I hoped he'd change his mind about wanting to keep things platonic. I loved him.

On the rare occasions we didn't sleep side by side, cuddling, it was because he'd deemed it inappropriate, without any warning. Sometimes a no-cuddling rule meant he was dating someone else. Sometimes it meant he just didn't feel like it.

During the weekend visits that involved those random boundaries, I felt broken up with all over again, so I did things to make him feel rejected, too. I'd zone out when he talked about his big accounting job so he knew I found it boring. I gave him backhanded compliments; I couldn't help myself.

Despite the dysfunctional state of our fraught friendship, Draco objected whenever I suggested we go our separate ways. He maintained that we were *best friends*, that our bond was unbreakable.

Once, long after we'd broken up, he told me we were the best couple he knew.

"But we're not a couple," I said.

"You know what I mean," he said. (I didn't.)

The natural implosion of our so-called best friendship occurred five years after our real breakup. I was going to a regular therapy appointment with Dr. Thomas and asked Draco if he wanted to come along.

"Sure," Draco said.

"It'll be great," I said. "We can talk about how we communicate."

We drove to Salem, ready to see Dr. Thomas, as if it were a common thing—two platonic friends seeking couples counseling.

Dr. Thomas stared us down in the office. He let us both rant for a bit about our problems as a twosome—and then he asked Draco a simple question.

"What is it that you want from your relationship with Meredith?"

"Well," Draco answered, making one of his many pensive Draco faces, "I always want to be her first phone call. I'd like us to meet other people, but I always want to be the first person she calls about important things."

His answer made me do a double take; for whatever reason, it was the wake-up smack in the face I needed.

"Um, I think I'd like my first phone call to be my mom," I told him. "Or maybe a real best friend like Jess who doesn't cuddle in bed with me. Or a real boyfriend who does."

Then I told him what so many of my friends had tried to tell me for years.

"This isn't going to work, because it's not good for me," I told Draco. "It's over."

Dr. Thomas looked pleased with himself, like he'd known this answer all along.

For a moment, as I watched Draco's face register that we were really breaking up, I felt horrible for him, because maybe he was losing *his* best friend. He didn't have a Jess or a Mark. We drove home from that appointment in silence, knowing it was a real goodbye.

After I made that decision, my exposure to Draco was minimal. I saw him at a friend's wedding, where I regressed and got drunk and said jealous things about his new relationship. A year or so later, when he married that woman, I saw pictures of the celebration because mutual friends posted them on Facebook. It hurt.

Draco and I had managed to avoid contacting each other for another five years—until I found an email from him in my *Globe* inbox. He wrote that he had plans to drive through Boston in a few weeks and wanted to meet for drinks or dinner.

The timing was weird because I'd been thinking so much about my letter writers and their friendships with exes.

I needed to get an outsider's opinion on my own situation, so I looked for Mark, but he wasn't there. I tried to think of who else in the building might have an opinion, and then I thought: Patrick. I found him in his office, next to his Larry Bird poster.

"That guy I dated in college emailed me and wants to get a drink," I told him.

"What does he want?" Patrick said, looking pleased that I had come to him for this conversation.

"The email says he'll be driving through Boston and wants to see me."

"Are you going to do it?"

"I don't know."

Patrick shrugged.

"From what you've told me, he sounds like a dickbag," he said.

"Yeah, maybe."

I'd missed that kind of Patrick talk so much; he always summed things up so well.

Then I called my mother for a second opinion.

"I don't think you should go," she said.

I could tell she was excited to be talking about something other than hospitals.

"I'm starting to think I *should* go," I said.

"But why?" my mom asked. "What would be the point?"

"Because I can," I explained. "I feel like saying no to Draco would suggest a weakness—that it would be too hard for me to have a meal with him. But I moved on from him so long ago. I can be his friend now."

"I don't know," my mom said, her voice scratchy. The new chemo pill she was trying made her cough a lot.

"I don't know what you could gain by having a friendship with Draco," she continued. "All I remember is that you guys brought out the worst in each other. You were kind of mean to each other. You didn't root for each other."

"It's just a meal," I said. "It's not a big deal."

I knew on some level that I would never tell a letter writer to have a friendly dinner with an ex just to prove they could. Still, I made plans to meet Draco.

I chose the Franklin Cafe in the South End—because I look really good there. *Everybody* looks good at the Franklin Cafe in the South End because the restaurant is so dark. There's a thick curtain by the door, so even in the summer you can sit at a table with circles under your eyes and food in your teeth and feel like a model.

Draco looked good there, too. On the night of our planned dinner, he sat across from me in a booth, nervous and happy to see me.

His hair was the same—he hadn't lost any. He was older, though, and didn't remind me of Draco Malfoy anymore. He looked like a grownup, with some flattering lines around his eyes.

We started the meal by talking about work. He updated me on his accounting business, and when I brought up the *Globe*, he admitted he'd been reading *Love Letters*.

I confessed that I'd written one of my early responses about him, and that I'd referred to him in the column as Draco Malfoy. This he hadn't known.

He could guess that the nickname was not a positive one, but he wasn't really a *Harry Potter* person, so he wasn't sure why.

"You're a lot like him," I said. "Don't be offended; he's a complicated character."

Draco said he'd heard from our mutual friends that my mom was sick, so I updated him about her treatment, trying to convey that I had it all under control, even though I was scared to death that I didn't. The situation sounded dire when summarized to someone out of the loop. I couldn't say "Stage 4" without clenching a fist.

"But you know," I said, "she's on this new pill that might shrink the metastases, which maybe means that the surgeons can go back in again and take the rest of them out. She's so strong. She bounces back from surgeries *so* easily."

"I'm really sorry you're going through this," Draco said. "I know how close you are."

"We'll be okay," I said. "Brette and I have got this."

Then Draco smiled. We both couldn't stop smiling, probably for the same reasons we were drawn to each other in college. I'd forgotten how his voice always sounded a little sarcastic in a way that I loved. He was so quick with a comeback, and always looked at me like I was the only other person on the planet. He was giving me that look in the Franklin Cafe. I wanted to crawl across the table.

The electricity rattled me, so I figured it was a good time to ask about his marriage.

"You guys must be thinking about kids," I said, trying to be breezy. "Is that something you want to do soon?"

"We're not thinking about kids right now," Draco said, shifting in his seat.

"I'm sorry; I never know if I should ask about that kind of thing," I said. "So many of my friends are having trouble conceiving. I should know that it's probably a rude question."

"We're not thinking about children at all right now," Draco said, his voice robotic.

"Okay," I said, "but how's it going otherwise? I haven't seen you since you got married. Tell me about it."

Draco looked at the ceiling.

"I'm getting a divorce," he said.

"What?"

"I'm getting a divorce," he repeated, pacing himself as I had when I'd shared my mom's diagnosis.

My stomach flipped.

"Is that why we're here?" I asked Draco, thinking of the timing of his request. "Is that why you emailed asking to see me?"

"No. I didn't know I was getting a divorce when I emailed you. This *just* happened. I just told my parents."

Draco took a labored breath and explained that it all started when he opened his email on his computer. It loaded his account automatically (or so he assumed), so he opened a message that looked like it was from his wife. What he found was a conversation between his wife and another man. He was confused until he realized he was in his wife's account. But it was too late—he'd seen suspicious content. He kept reading messages until he confirmed that she was having an affair.

In Draco's case, the cheating he found was worse than the snoop. He confronted his wife and she confirmed the betrayal. Just a few years into the marriage, she wanted out. He asked her to leave their house in Connecticut.

It had all gone down about two weeks prior to our dinner. Draco had barely started processing what it meant for his future.

"Are you sure it's really over?" I asked. "You could work it out. Couples can survive infidelity. People make mistakes."

"It's over," Draco said. "There's no going back."

The Franklin Cafe server delivered a bowl of mussels in tomato broth. I picked at the bread, uncomfortable with the silence and how Draco seemed to be gazing at the table, stunned by everything he'd shared.

"I didn't expect to talk about this," he said. "I didn't expect to tell you."

"You know," I said, "I see this issue a lot in my column—cheating and snooping. It's very common."

I kept talking; trite advice columnist things were flying out of my mouth by the second.

"I'm so sorry," I said, finally, when I realized he wasn't looking for me to fix it. "I'm just so sorry."

And I *was* sorry, which surprised me a little.

I had been miserable when I'd seen Draco's wedding pictures on Facebook, and I'll admit that one percent of me—the *worst* one percent of me—had hoped his marriage would fail. That horrible selfish part of my brain wished, back in the day, that Draco would wind up single and seeking out my attention under the low lights of a place like the Franklin Cafe. I'd fantasized about this kind of dinner.

Now that it was actually happening, though, no part of me could celebrate his heartache. He went on to tell me that he and his wife had been planning to have kids. He thought he'd be a dad soon, and now he was starting over.

Our dinner lasted more than two hours, and he said we should keep in touch. He wanted to be friends.

I said I would consider it, but it felt like a bad idea. I still cared too much.

As I walked away from the restaurant, I texted Patrick.

"I just hung out with that guy from college," I wrote. "It was weird."

"Where are you now?" he asked.

"In the South End."

He wrote back that he was at a bar nearby. "Come on over."

I almost ran there.

He was with some of the friends I'd never met when we were dating. I was happy not to have known them then, because now Patrick could introduce me as what I was.

"This is my friend Meredith," he said. The label didn't sound horrible.

We all hung out and talked, and then Patrick walked me to my car, which was still parked in an outdoor lot near the Franklin. We stood in front of my Hyundai enjoying the fact that it was almost spring—not as frigid as it had been for so many months.

"I want to tell you something, Patrick," I said, my head craned upward because he was so tall.

"Sure," Patrick said, looking down, his eyes glassy from an evening of drinking.

"I feel like the problem with Draco and me being friends is that we didn't know how to root for each other," I said, quoting my mother. "Draco and I were competitive with each other. And sometimes we loved each other too much—in a way that made it impossible for either of us to move on… But you and I are always rooting for each other, and we've always been great at giving each other space. I want to be part of your happiness, even if I'm not the center of it."

Patrick's smile got bigger.

"Yep," he said.

Then we hugged, his long arms wrapped around me, and I didn't want to kiss him at all.

READY FOR A FRIENDSHIP WITH AN EX?

Q. I dated a guy for four months. He ended things by saying that he didn't see a future with me. I was sad but not angry, and we ended things on relatively good terms. Two months later, he called. We had a catch-up session and then he asked me out for drinks/dinner. I explained that I really couldn't be friends, not yet, not as long as I still harbored feelings. He suggested checking back in a month. A few weeks went by and I caved. I thought I was in a place to handle being a friend. I wasn't. We got in a fight because of my emotional wishy-washiness, and never made it to even planning drinks.

I had assumed the worst of his intentions—loneliness or guilt. In reality, he genuinely wanted to be friends (he has a strong track record of friendships with exes to support his intentions). It ended on less than stellar terms. He was hurt. I felt bad. I apologized, but the damage was already done. Now, months later, I would like to be his friend and think I can be a friend. Only thing is, I don't know how to approach him. I fear the door may be permanently closed. Any ideas?

—Hopefully a Friend

A. If the guy can't forgive you for having a tough time adjusting to a friendship, he's not good friend material. You can't dump someone and then demand that they become your friend on *your* schedule. Why isn't he worried about how this friendship might confuse you? Why is he focused on his own pain instead of yours?

My advice is to spend some time thinking about what you'd really get out of a friendship. Can you be around him without having romantic feelings for him? What does he offer as a platonic companion?

If you think this through and still want him around as a pal, just give him a call. If he's really capable of a good friendship, he'll give this another shot and try it on your terms. If he doesn't respond well or makes this all about him, please leave that door closed.

—Meredith

READERS? WHAT DO YOU THINK?

Is he considered an "ex" after only four months? I feel he's more in the "someone I dated" category. — MINGUSTRANE

I don't remember ever thinking that being rejected by someone was a solid foundation for a friendship. — MOVA

Burning bridges is the most fun part of a breakup. Why waste it? — SKYWARP94

STILL HAVE FEELINGS FOR AN EX AND CO-PARENT

Q. From reading your column daily over the past few years, I see that both you and your readers always advise against exes remaining friends if one still has romantic feelings for the other. I understand it's not healthy to remain in that type of platonic relationship, and most of the responses I've seen on the subject say to simply cut ties. But what if there are young children and shared custody involved? The parents really have no choice but to see each other at least twice per week. How does the parent who still has feelings for the other deal with this situation?

—Still Love My Ex, Brookline

A. I wouldn't say that we (the royal *Love Letters* we) always recommend cutting ties with exes. We just want people to protect themselves. We certainly don't want anyone to pretend to be platonic pals with an ex when they're really pining for a second chance.

When kids are involved, exes need to maintain a civil relationship, which is very different from a full-blown platonic friendship. You should be cordial, loving co-parents—not part-time life partners. You can call each other to talk about the kids, but you shouldn't be checking in late at night when you're watching TV and just want to chat.

The goal is to find other people to call when you get those

lonely feelings. It can take years to establish boundaries with an ex, but if you obey your own rules and lean on other people for companionship, you'll train yourself to compartmentalize.

Try to make the most of your nights off from the kids by seeing friends and building a rich life. That's the best (and maybe only) way to feel better about an ex and keep the relationship in perspective.

—Meredith

READERS? WHAT DO YOU THINK?

Meredith's advice is spot on today! You should treat your ex civilly but maintain an almost businesslike relationship related to the kids only. I don't chitchat with my ex about my life, regardless of how friendly we are now. We talk about our son and that's it. — LILY

My experience has been that the best way to get over someone is to find someone else. I know that sounds like awful advice—but I don't mean falling madly in love, moving in with someone else type of thing. I simply mean, date someone, discover another person who values you. Or even a couple of people. Don't allow yourself to be defined by the ex. — MOLLYSINGS

Maybe he is feeling the same way you do. If neither of you are out there dating then maybe it is worth another shot. Sometimes you don't know what you got until it is gone. — BZZNABOUT

Chapter 12

Sickness and Health

I wound up at Facing Cancer Together because of my friend Jenn, a Spotlight reporter at the *Globe*. She made me go.

She demanded that I sign up for the organization's caregivers support group because she saw that I was anxious and twitchy and that the smaller lines on my forehead were becoming ravines.

She probably also noticed that I wasn't washing my hair as much, and that all grooming, in general, had gone to shit. I'd stopped tweezing the one weird gray hair growing out of the side of my face because it would just grow back, and the cycle exhausted me.

Every minute felt wrong. If I was spending time with my mom, taking her to dinners and movies or doctors' appointments, I felt bad about not being more engaged at work. When I was concentrating on work, I felt bad that I wasn't spending time with my mom.

No matter what I was doing, I felt bad that I wasn't advancing my personal life—no dates, no flirtations. I had become a distracted friend. I missed my friend Brad's wedding because the thought of being around that many people at once seemed too difficult. I owed people emails.

I liked to go to Jess's house because she didn't force me to engage. Also, it's cool to see a great friend become an incredible parent.

Less than two years after having her first son, Alex, she'd had another son, Gabe. Jess would watch over both kids, sometimes while pumping breast milk, as I sat in front of the television, zoning out in front of episodes of the Canadian children's cartoon *Caillou* (even though *Caillou* is the worst), and a British-American kids' cartoon, *Chloe's Closet*, which is about a young Welsh girl who brings her young friends into her closet to have imaginary adventures.

"Do you think it's a metaphor?" Jess would ask, trying to keep me laughing.

"The closet? Maybe. Just maybe. A really subtle metaphor," I said, relieved that we were talking about something easy and stupid, even though Jess knew what was on my mind.

Just being close to Jess and a television made things feel a little easier.

My mom had been sick for three years, and our expectations for her future had changed, even though we rarely talked about it. Every few months we went to Mass General for a scan, and every result was just a little worse than the one before. The tiny metastases in her lungs grew slightly larger. Things were always going in the wrong direction.

"Basically inconsequential growth," my mom's doctor would say. "It's such a small growth that we *don't even count it* as growth," he'd sometimes add, which made us feel better for about fifteen seconds.

What became clear during these appointments was that her cancer wasn't going to shrink, and that "status quo" was the best it would get. There was no more talk of another lung surgery to clear out the cancer. A new chemo pill was slowing the growth of the disease, but she'd be on the drug—or something like it—for the rest of her life.

The doctor did say it was possible that my mom could exist as she was for years, maybe decades, and that sounded great to Brette and me. My mom's quality of life was sometimes wonderful, despite the cancer; even at her most exhausted, she exercised more than I did, and was still up for walking around the city and big meals out.

She loved taking the T and spending the afternoon at the Museum of Fine Arts. With the chemo pill, her neuropathy faded, and she was able to sit at her Steinway, practicing while she waited for me to finish with work so we could go to dinner.

I just wished she could enjoy her retirement without having to tie it to the sickness. Fun dinners out could so easily turn into me rushing her home because of gastrointestinal flare-ups—a reminder of why she was in Boston to begin with. Sometimes during those trips to the Museum of Fine Arts, she would call me at the office, panicked about what would happen if the chemo stopped working.

"Tell me it'll be okay," she'd beg.

"It will be," I'd say, because I couldn't come up with any other response.

"Do you think I'm going to die?" she'd ask, her voice high like a toddler's.

"Well, like, *eventually* you're going to die," I'd say, trying to cut the tension with sarcasm. "We're *all* going to die. But not anytime soon."

My mother wasn't the stoic sick parent you see in movies—like Meryl Streep in *One True Thing*, where she's still a supermom and tries to decorate an entire town for Christmas. She wasn't behaving like Susan Sarandon in *Stepmom*, where the sick mom character gets super cool and smokes pot and cracks sarcastic jokes. My mom was still the same mom I'd always known—peer-like and needing advice, which meant she looked to me for constant validation.

It was a good time to become an even better friend to my mother than I'd ever been—to boost her spirits as she accepted her limited future. I wanted to be the perfect companion and cheerleader, the daughter who made everything better.

The only problem was that my mother had become the most annoying person on the planet.

I wanted to yell at her all the time.

No matter what kind of friendship we had, we were still mother and daughter, which meant she often did and said things that made me want to scream "UGH, STOP TALKING, MOM," like I was fourteen.

Like when she said "get on internet" instead of "get on *the* internet." She made that mistake a lot.

"I'm going to get on internet and google some restaurants," she'd say.

I'd have to hold back from shouting "*THE* INTERNET—

YOU'RE GOING TO GET ON *THE* INTERNET," because I knew it would make her feel bad.

Or when she said "tread" instead of "treadmill," like her treadmill needed a nickname.

"I'm just going to walk on the tread to get some exercise," she'd say to me or to Brette, who'd also reached her limit with my mother's shorthand.

"*MILL*," Brette and I would yell to each other during late-night calls. "TREAD. FUCKING. MILL. Why can't she say the whole word?"

We could have made a dictionary of my mom's abbreviations and malapropisms, which were only exacerbated by the chemo that fogged her brain. The most annoying mistake she repeated during this time was "Edna Farber." She always called Boston's Dana-Farber Cancer Institute the "Edna Farber"—maybe because of writer Edna Ferber?—and I'd yell "DANA!" and then she'd look wounded because I'd made her feel stupid, and then I'd feel like a terrible person because I'd yelled at my mother with Stage 4 cancer, so I'd be nice until the next time she did it, and then the cycle would begin again.

(I should mention that my mother wasn't being treated at the Dana-Farber. We were always at Mass General. Still, she managed to find reasons to say Edna Farber—a lot.)

On my worst days, I said things to Brette like, "We have to get Mom better—so we can kill her."

I couldn't make that kind of joke to my friends, because it was awful and not funny, and I thought no one but Brette would understand.

Except for the people at Facing Cancer Together.

At the caregivers support group meetings, I quickly learned that Brette and I weren't the only terrible people who wanted to say awful things about our sick loved ones. It was a place where tired family members and spouses could admit that their partners still pissed them off, even though they were ill.

The group leader, a young guy who always looked a little afraid of us, reminded us, in his soft support-group voice, that we were not bad people for having terrible thoughts about the people we loved. "Under great stress, why wouldn't small annoyances seem even bigger?" he asked.

It was this validating question that inspired me to keep attending the group, even though it was just one more thing I'd have to add to my schedule. I got the sense it wasn't easy for any of the caregivers to get the support we needed; Facing Cancer Together was housed in a small white church in a suburb west of Boston, a tough drive during rush hour, which was when the group met every week. By the time all of the caregivers arrived, parked, and used the bathroom, we looked annoyed and haggard, because making that trip was stress on top of stress.

I decided early on to try to stay quiet during our sessions, mostly because of who I was in the group. Of the ten or so members, I was the only caregiver who was the child of a patient, as opposed to a spouse or parent. Most of the other caregivers were tending to wives who'd been diagnosed with breast cancer in their forties, or young husbands with rare forms of myeloma and brain cancer.

That's why I felt like I should just listen—because who was I to complain? I was a single woman in my thirties with no kids and no real responsibilities outside of my job. I didn't live with my mom, which meant I always got a break.

I had to acknowledge right off the bat that even though my mom had Stage 4 cancer, she was still healthy enough to eat an entire carrot cake and to go see Sting with the *Globe*'s music critic. Some of these people had it so much worse.

I was also more comfortable listening in the group because it reminded me of reading people's problems for *Love Letters*. Like my letter writers, who shared so much, these caregivers opened up about what it was like to see their partners at their worst, how they cleaned up bodily fluids while getting yelled at by sick loved ones who couldn't help but lash out at their closest companion. The caregivers ranted about their in-laws and confessed that sometimes all they wanted to do was watch seventeen hours of television and not talk to anyone. Mostly I just nodded.

Sometimes when I got home after group, I thought about things I'd wanted to say—what I would have talked about had I not felt like an impostor.

My biggest stress at the time, beyond the illness itself, was money. I was spending a lot of it.

When we needed a U-Haul to move my mom from Maryland to Boston, that went on a credit card. Concert tickets for a band she really liked? Credit card. In the mood for spaghetti? We'd go to the fanciest Italian restaurant I could find, and I'd put it on a credit card.

My mom never had extra money; she managed to keep us in our suburban house after the divorce by teaching piano into the night, sometimes six days a week. She was frugal enough to keep up with families with two incomes, which meant that Brette and I never skipped school trips or dropped our music lessons.

But she rarely spent any money on herself. She tried to keep even the basics to a minimum. Sometimes she kept the lights off when we were kids because she said she "liked the dark," but I knew she was trying to save on the electricity bill.

Brette and I didn't grow up to be savers like her—we liked treating ourselves to meals and trips, at the expense of our savings—and once my mom got sick, we became even bigger spenders, now for her. We decided that for every bad experience in the hospital—for every time she got stabbed with a needle or had to sit through a scan—my mom was entitled to an incredible, unforgettable experience. Brette and I were like a Make-A-Wish Foundation for just one person.

We liked to end our Mass General trips with a meal at Scampo in the nearby Liberty Hotel. It's a lovely restaurant where you can spend twenty-seven dollars for one mozzarella tasting plate. Out came our credit cards.

I bought her a Kindle Fire, which seemed fancy at the time, so she could watch *Parks and Recreation* marathons during treatment, and kept loading the thing with books and other entertainment. I always parked in the stupid thirty-dollar parking lots whenever we went out so she wouldn't have to walk far if it was cold.

Credit card, credit card, credit card. The little things were adding up.

Brette often went even bigger with her gifts, especially when my mom stayed with her in New York City. One night, Brette surprised her with tickets to see a fancy clarinet player who was performing at a chamber music festival at Carnegie Hall. Brette ordered a big car to get them there. Mom was ecstatic.

Meanwhile, Brette was turning down one casting job after another so she could come to Boston for medical appointments and procedures. She was losing income as fast as she was spending it.

My mom wasn't oblivious to this—she'd sometimes ask, "Is this affordable? Do you have enough money?"—but we always made it seem like it wasn't a big deal. "This is why I don't have kids," I'd say, with a laugh. "More disposable income for me!"

I knew my mom was living off the money she made by selling her house. I could tell she was stressed about that, and I didn't want her to dip into that account more than she needed to.

In the caregivers support group, where I was supposed to be able to air all of my fears, I wanted to ask how Brette and I could keep up the spending, but I couldn't bring myself to share the problem. Some of the other caregivers in the circle were balancing medical bills, crazy mortgages, and feeding many children. Brette and I had only ourselves to blame for our spiraling debt and our mom's expectations. Instead of coming clean to my mom—or to the group—I looked for credit cards with more points and lower interest rates. I told myself I'd do the math later. Maybe the *Globe* would be bought by Google and we'd get stock options.

Had I more courage, I would have also told the group how Brette and I had stopped taking care of ourselves. I began to rely on food delivery for all meals at home and had gained enough weight from pad thai that my boobs had started to muffin top over my bra. Mark and I called the extra layer of boob "second boob" because it looked like I had four boobs in total.

Brette, meanwhile, was ignoring her Crohn's disease diet and consumed all the gluten she could find. The inflammation in her knees was so bad that she was walking like my grandpa Marty.

We also behaved horribly when we were alone together. We felt entitled and enjoyed the things we liked in excess. Those "things" included pills and wine. Sometimes those pills were not prescribed to us.

One night, after a particularly stressful afternoon with my mother that involved a scan result, my sister and I took Benadryl and oxycodone (I did not ask where my sister found this oxycodone, but I imagined it was from my mother's surgeries), and then split a bottle of Riesling. I intended on having a small glass of wine, but we kept refilling our cups until the bottle was gone.

I went to bed feeling incredible, unencumbered and calm for once—until I woke up covered in sweat, my heart pounding like a bass drum in my chest. I called Brette into my bedroom; she'd been on the couch, still awake, watching television.

"What's up?" she asked.

"I'm sweating and my heart is beating fast, and I might be having a bad reaction to the oxycodone and wine," I said.

"Um, do you think we should go to the hospital?" Brette asked, still relaxed and clearly high from the medication.

"I really don't want to," I said.

"Well, like, do you think you're *dying*?" Brette asked.

"Unclear," I said.

Brette went to the living room to get her laptop. She came back and placed it on her legs, and then googled "symptoms of death."

"Ugh, I don't want to go to the hospital," I moaned, "but Mom will totally kill us if I die from taking pills and drinking wine."

"Yeah, that's the last thing she needs," Brette agreed.

Google was little help. We decided to wait it out, and eventually we both fell asleep. We woke up admitting that we needed to do better, but I can't say that's the last time we indulged.

I could have used the group's help, because I'm sure some of my fellow caregivers had found their own irresponsible ways to escape. Maybe they would have been able to tell me how to cope without putting myself at risk.

Had I felt comfortable talking about my advice column in that group, I also would have admitted that my personal life was affecting my work. In one instance, a woman who was a breast cancer survivor had written in to tell me she was annoyed that her husband didn't want to have sex with her. Now that she was healthy, he wasn't interested, and she couldn't understand why her husband had shut down the minute that she was ready to live the rest of her life.

I responded with a rant about how she needed to give her husband a break. He'd been strong for her, and now she had to let him take some space for himself. My answer was so transparent that my mom, who still read the column first thing every morning, brought it up at one of our dinners and began to cry.

"Was that a message to me?" she asked, her lips trembling.

"Of course not," I said. "It's a letter from a wife about her sex life with her husband. How could that have anything to do with us?"

I went back and looked at the letter and my response, and

I was horrified. I had projected my exhaustion and resentment all over the letter writer. I assumed so much about the letter writer's husband that to anyone who knew me, it was clear I was talking about myself.

I thought about apologizing to my mother and talking it through, but I didn't.

It was too strange of an issue to bring up in my support group, I decided, so I kept it to myself.

♡

The one issue I did bring up in the group was dating. One evening, when the leader asked for an update, I told my fellow caregivers that I didn't think I could date while my mom was ill, which meant that the longer she lived, the longer I'd be single.

I didn't know how to meet someone new without talking about my mom's cancer. What else mattered?

The group had some advice and did what commenters do: They became an in-person message board of strangers who knew almost nothing about me but had an opinion anyway.

I tried to imagine what their screen names would be if they were on *Love Letters*. There was WomanWhoDoesn'tBelieve-CancerPatientsShouldTakeAntiDepressants, GuyWhoHatesHis-InLaws, WomanWho'sAnnoyedWeForgetHowToPronounceMye-loma.

I didn't know them, not really, but I trusted them the same way I trusted my readers.

They told me not to bring up my mom's cancer on a first date, if I could get one, and they helped me think of other things to talk about. They admitted they were baffled by the question because they were all married and agreed it must be overwhelming to even think about getting to know someone new during this kind of life-or-death struggle.

"It's okay to not date at all," one said.

"But maybe I *want* to date somebody," I admitted. "And if she keeps living—like this, at least—I can't."

No one had answers, but it felt good to say it all out loud.

❦

My support group experience didn't last long. After a few months, the members of my particular circle decided to disband.

My group leader attributed it to the fact that one member's husband died shortly after our sessions began. The loss was so jarring and scary that the rest of us never quite rallied. It made the rest of us feel as though our little club was simply a stepping-stone to the bereavement support group, which met down the hall.

I was told about the disbanding of our group while on vacation with my mom in Ireland (credit card). She'd never been there, and it's an easy flight from Boston, so we spent a week touring the sights.

We stayed in Dublin and Galway, and she fell in love with the Aran Islands because people built tiny homes for imaginary fairies next to their houses. My mom took many pictures of those miniature homes, like she was thinking about shrinking herself and living in one.

I understood why she was drawn to them; Ireland, in general, felt like a place where there might be magic cures.

The group leader left me a voicemail while I was on the islands; he said we'd no longer be meeting, but that Facing Cancer Together offered other services if I needed them. I didn't call back, mainly because the thought of trying again overwhelmed me. Also, I got one big thing I needed from the experience.

I learned that even if it was many years in the future, I *would* graduate to the bereavement group.

I don't think I'd admitted that to myself until then.

SEX AFTER CANCER

Q. I have been a longtime reader. Really enjoy everyone's input.

I've been married for almost ten years. Right after we were married, I was diagnosed with breast cancer. I was in my thirties and was devastated. After multiple surgeries (including a mastectomy), chemo, and radiation, we started to build our married life. We were blessed to have two beautiful children. After my second child, my remaining breast started showing "signs" of potential breast cancer. Over the next year, I had two biopsies and multiple mammograms. Emotionally, this tipped me over the edge and I had the remaining breast removed.

My issue? Since my last surgery three years ago, my husband refuses to have "marital relations" with me. No touching. No nothing. I mean NOTHING!!!! A peck in the morning to say goodbye and a peck in the evening to say good night. A few "I love yous" throughout the day. I understand for men breasts are very important. I miss them also. I've tried to approach the topic and his response is "we need to schedule a time." Well, with two children, it's difficult to schedule a time. Counseling? He owns his own business and works seven days a week. He feels he doesn't have time to go. And, no, he isn't cheating on me.

I love my husband but I can't remain in a non-physical marriage. It's lonely. He knows I'm not happy but he feels that the marriage is okay. Well, it's not. I hate ultimatums but I don't know what else do to. Meredith... Readers... Help!

—Breastless in Massachusetts

A. This isn't about his busy schedule, and it's not about your breasts. It's about the whole ordeal.

When someone gets cancer, their family and friends often become a full-time support group. And when it's over—if things work out for the best—there's this massive sigh of relief, and everyone tries to go back to their normal lives as best they can.

That's fine, except for the fact that the main caregivers are still emotionally exhausted. They've used up all of their energy to help their loved ones (and themselves) get through the experience. Sometimes they're not just tired, they're angry. Irrational or not, sometimes they're furious with their formerly sick loved one for unintentionally putting them through so much. And no matter what, they're panicked that the illness will return.

There's a lot of literature out there about sex after cancer—that caregiver spouses are afraid of accidentally hurting their partner physically by taking part in sexual activity, or worse, hurting their partner's feelings if they have a negative reaction to their new body. That could be a part of his problem: fear.

There's less literature out there that adequately describes the emotional crash that happens after years of compartmentalizing a very scary thing.

You've asked him for support for years and now you're asking for something else. He's having trouble understanding that this request is supposed to be a fun one. I think he's still shell-shocked.

I'd start slow—with cuddling. Sit close to him in front of the television or offer up a back rub. See if you can move it along from there over time.

No matter how he responds to PG touching, he has to make time for therapy—probably without you. You can tell him that a lack of interest in sex after cancer is very normal—and fixable. He'll probably be relieved to hear that he's not a horrible jerk for wanting to avoid it after all that you've been through.

Assure him that you'll watch the kids while he takes an hour to talk to a professional or, better yet, a cancer support group (of which there are many). Do this with a loving smile on your face. Remind him that your marriage is "okay" only if you both think it is.

And maybe plan a vacation. Get some of those supportive friends to watch the kids. The more new memories you make that don't involve waiting for the results of a PET scan, the better it will be for both of you.

—Meredith

READERS? WHAT DO YOU THINK?

My boyfriend was diagnosed with prostate cancer after we had been dating for nine months. My boyfriend is fine now, but it really affected our relationship. We both had an underlying fear of the cancer getting worse, and his dying. It affected our relationship in a lot of bad ways. At

one point, we almost broke up. We love each other very much, so rather than lose each other we made a commitment to talk about our fears, what was bothering us, and how our behavior had changed. That was over a year ago. It was hard, and we had some bad times, but slowly we've become closer than ever. — NYLADY01

I finished all of my cancer treatments in February and my relationship with my husband is nothing like it was before my diagnosis. My cancer didn't affect any part of the female anatomy, but we do have a near loveless relationship almost EXACTLY like yours. I agree with Meredith, perhaps he's feeling that I unintentionally put him through so much, is panicked that the cancer will return and feeling he may accidentally hurt me near the incision during sex (I am still very tender). I believe he IS still shell-shocked. I have forgotten so much of what went on and have a bright outlook, but he was there to see me in all my pain and suffering during chemo and radiation, almost dying several times right in front of him, extremely difficult surgeries and a high rate of the cancer to spread. All that is still in his memory as he was SEEING it all happen—I just lived through it. There are efforts being made on his part as well as mine. We are making slow strides. Perhaps you could show him some of this column and ask him to be your partner in strengthening your bond and recommitting to the health of your marriage. — EDU–GIRL

Chapter 13

Ring Watch

The first time "ring watch" was mentioned in the column was in January of 2013. The phrase was used by a woman who wrote in to confess that she was on track to get married, even though she had major doubts about her relationship.

"This pang of insecurity started lingering maybe a year ago, but I just attributed it to being too young to get married," she wrote. "Now that I am officially at an age where I thought it would be appropriate to count down the months on ring watch, it's become more serious."

Readers latched on to the phrase "ring watch" because it seemed like a good way to describe another kind of letter we'd seen over the years. So many of our questions came from people who felt pressure to lock down their relationships. They were on a path to a prize and wanted public confirmation.

For the record, most ring-watch letters were submitted to the column in January. I assumed that was because so many people had expected proposals around Christmas and New Year's, and when no questions were popped, there was anger—then, later, a letter to an advice columnist.

The *Love Letters* audience saw "ring watch" as a bad thing. The concept suggested a prioritization of trinkets and rituals over real partnership.

But to me, the concepts didn't have to be mutually exclusive. I'd never had any interest in weddings, marriage, or hand accessories (rings often give me eczema), but I understood that those things were important symbols of a shared life. I didn't think it was bad to be on ring watch, or to want to know the deal had been sealed.

Again, it was my sister who helped me figure this out.

♥

Brette had never been an expensive-jewelry or weddings person, either, but once she fell in love with Ben, she was on ring watch, too. What had started as a maybe-fling with a ten-year age gap had turned into something serious over the years. Ben was still living with Brette in New York City. They got along well, and my sister was sure Ben was the one—or, to be more accurate, the one she wanted.

Ben wasn't sure, though, and that made sense. He was entering his late twenties while Brette was planning for forty.

"He has to shit or get off the pot," Brette would say to my mom and me, on the phone or in person after my mom's hospital visits. Sometimes she'd yell or whisper the words at various decibels and speeds. "Shit. Or. Get. Off. The. Pot. *Shitorgetoffthepot.*"

Ben understood Brette's drive to start planning the rest of

her life. He also knew that my mom's illness had forced her to ask big questions about the future. If he wasn't in it for sickness and health—for all of it, really—Brette deserved to know so she could look for someone else.

Ben also wanted a big commitment—someday—but he feared that if he married the person he'd met in his mid-twenties, he'd have regrets years down the road.

"What else do you want to experience before you get married?" Brette would ask whenever he explained his reservations. "Sleeping with other women?"

Most likely the name "Katya" floated through her brain.

"Maybe?" Ben admitted. "And I always thought that maybe I'd live in California for a few years."

"Couldn't we live in California *together*?" Brette asked.

"I guess," Ben said.

But that wasn't the point. Ben pictured being in California on his own.

"You know what? Go," Brette said with biting sarcasm. "Go to California. Stay with your hippie glassblower friends. Enjoy."

This argument was frequent and only ended when they agreed to table the issue until they were ready to fight again. It was just like my letter writers who often went in circles with their partners about whether to break up or get married, because for many long-term couples, there was no in-between anymore.

I was on Ben's side, to the extent that I could be. I told Brette it was unfair to expect Ben to have final answers in his mid-twenties, because in her mid-twenties, she was nowhere close to settling down. Had she been forced into making a decision about marriage back then, she would have chosen to remain single, no matter what.

"But I hadn't met the right person in my mid-twenties," Brette argued. "I don't think I would have let the right person get away."

My mom sided with Brette, at least about it being time for Ben to make a choice.

"He can do whatever he wants, but he can't have her waiting around for years," my mom said. "She's almost forty. If he's not in this relationship for the long run, she needs to know."

"Exactly," Brette agreed whenever my mom made that point. "He can get off the pot if he wants. He just can't hover over it, pretending he might eventually shit."

Brette didn't *need* a wedding, she said. She wasn't obsessed with getting a certain kind of ring. But she did *want* both of those things because she believed they were symbols of his intentions. They meant something to him and to the world, and maybe to his family. Having the promise, as well as those signs and rites of passage, meant it was real.

I wondered whether Ben would be more comfortable making a big commitment if it didn't involve a proposal. My friends Jenn (from work) and Paul (from college)—whom I'd set up in their early twenties—were still together more than a decade later and had never been interested in marriage. I believed their success was tied to the fact that they'd never had a shit-or-get-off-the-pot moment. They'd just kept living together, day after day, planning for the future with the best intentions. Over time, their commitment became clear. They'd invested in the same property and cared for each other's families. They agreed that if one moved, the other would follow. It felt organic, partly because there'd never been any ultimatums or deadlines.

"We have a house and we share families, so what's the difference?" Jenn once said. "Plus, we've seen couples get married and divorced in the time we've been together. It's not like marriage is a guarantee."

Brette said that was all well and good for Jenn and Paul because they'd started dating in their early twenties. They had years to grow into their relationship, so by the time they needed to ask bigger questions, they had answers. Brette had a point.

I didn't know whether Ben's intentions could ever match Brette's. It was clear that he loved her, but in his heart, he had concerns about forever.

My mom and I braced ourselves for the possibility that Brette might have to let go and start over. Like many of my letter writers, she'd already set a few ultimatums, but she let them pass. Now it was an unspoken thing between them; he knew what she wanted, and that at some point, she'd tell him it was over. The waiting and unmet expectations were poisoning their great relationship by the day.

But eventually there was a decision.

One random afternoon—when the issue was still hanging over their heads—Ben took a long walk around New York City. The point of the journey, he later said, was to make peace with the reality of his relationship—and what he needed to let go. He knew it was time.

He wandered the East Village and then returned to the apartment where Brette was on the couch, waiting to go to the bathroom.

She had a colonoscopy scheduled for the next morning (she had them often because of her Crohn's disease, and now because of my mother's illness), so she was in gastrointestinal purgatory, waiting for the prep solution to tear through her system.

Ben knew it probably wasn't fair to have the conversation while her stomach was in knots—his timing was terrible—but he had to come clean in his own way, and it couldn't wait. He was ready to accept the fate of their relationship.

He let her know that when it came to his own pot, he had decided—figuratively—to shit.

"Will you marry me?" Ben said.

"Are you sure?" Brette asked.

"Yes," Ben said.

"Me too," Brette answered.

Then Brette picked up her phone, walked to the bathroom, and called my mom and me while having explosive diarrhea.

Later, I tried to get to the bottom of what Ben discovered on his walk—how he got his brain around the idea of lifelong commitment. I wanted to know what he told himself, and how he made peace with forgoing other experiences, like whatever he imagined would happen in California.

I hoped there was an easy explanation, something I could boil down for my readers, so they could put their ring watches to rest.

But Ben wasn't able to give me a real answer. He said he knew he loved my sister and that they had a really good time together. He used the word "lucky," which, to me, said a lot.

Ultimately, when it came down to two choices, breaking up or staying together, one option seemed like a lot more fun. That much he knew.

SHOULD I GIVE UP ON MARRIAGE?

Q. Hi Mere! I have been with "Dave" for three years now, living together for two and a half and very happy. We have had our ups and downs but we are both happy.

Now here is the issue: I want to get married. I'm not in a hurry, but eventually I want that form of commitment from him. I am twenty-seven years old, from a large Irish-Catholic family/background, so growing up, marriage seemed like a natural next step. Now, I am well aware that marriages don't always turn out happily ever after and many people live their lives with their partner anyway. That being said, I'd still like to be married…not to just anyone, but to Dave.

Dave does not share my viewpoint. He's thirty-seven and feels that weddings are too much hassle and that "you don't need a piece of paper to be happy and to show commitment." I believe that his experience with his parents may have something to do with this. (He's an only child, parents still married but fought a lot. They admitted that they stayed married for him when he was young. They are still together and happier from what I've been told.) I come from a family of divorce and still think that with work and love, a marriage can be successful.

I have told him what I want and he's still very hesitant, flip-flopping between not being financially ready and not needing the piece of paper. I am torn. I want to spend my life with him (not just anyone, so please no one think that I am just looking for a ring), but I want a marriage and I need this piece of paper, I guess. I'm at the point where I'm being asked on a daily basis when I'm getting engaged, and it's weighing on me. Should I just give up and be unmarried with the love of my life or should I make it clear what I want out of life and not compromise? Am I being selfish in wanting more? Should I accept that I will have a permanent boyfriend? Thanks for everyone's help!

—Always the Girlfriend, Worcester

A. It's okay to want the piece of paper. If the legal document is something you need, you must talk to your boyfriend about a compromise. Maybe he'd be open to marriage if you skip the big wedding.

Is there a way to remove the financial pressure from the request?

It sounds like you haven't articulated why you need the piece of paper (beyond the family obligation stuff) and how a marriage might change the relationship. Perhaps you should sit down with your boyfriend (yes, again) and talk about where you'd like to be in five years. Does he anticipate that you'll still be together? With a family? If so, how would marriage help/change that experience?

This doesn't seem to be about ring watch. And it shouldn't be about people asking you when you're getting engaged (please tell them to mind their own business).

Marriage is about living and planning as a team. So ask your boyfriend: What is the plan? And more importantly, What's best for both of you?

—Meredith

READERS? WHAT DO YOU THINK?

Sorry, but you shouldn't compromise. You should be clear. This is a deal breaker...and stop calling him the love of your life. He's only the love of your life up until this point. — SEXUALCHOCOLATE

You will have to decide what is more important to you—marriage or Dave. That said, he does sound like he's vacillating a little bit. If you can explain to him why marriage is important and what it means to you, he might see your point. Not wanting to get married, not *needing* to be married, and not being ready for marriage are all different things. And tell your nosy relatives to butt out. What they want is least important. — WIZEN

Holy hell, did I write this letter? Letter writer, let me know what you learn here. I don't think I can help you today. — STELLAZ

SHE WANTS TO PROPOSE TO HER BOYFRIEND

Q. My question is fairly simple: Is it okay for a woman to propose to a man? My boyfriend and I are in a very loving, committed, and fun relationship, and I feel as though it is more of an equal partnership than one with traditional gender roles.

We have discussed our plans for the future, and we know marriage and a family are on the horizon. He (and I) have been saving up for a ring and wedding, but he would like to have all the money saved up before he proposes. We both have student loans we are still paying off.

I understand his reasoning, but I have told him that I do not care about a ring or a big extravagant wedding. I believe he feels the pressure (not from me) to get a big diamond, do a big proposal, and then a big wedding. He wants to do it "right." The more I think about it, the more I want to propose to him. I already have a plan, and I just need to pull the trigger. Is that okay for a woman to do? Even if we are equals in this relationship, would I be stepping on his toes? What's the downside of going forward with my plans?

I would love to get some male perspective on this. I have discussed this with a couple of my close girlfriends—and they have said not to do it for LOTS of different reasons. Guys, how would you feel if your girlfriend proposed to you? Would you say yes? Thanks in advance for any advice (and encouragement!) you can give.

—Will You Be My Husband?

A. There's nothing wrong with a woman proposing to a man. But in your case, your boyfriend has made it clear that he wants to do this a certain way. His version of getting it "right" means buying a big ring and probably getting down on one knee. How do you think he'd feel if you took that away from him?

People surprise each other with proposals all of the time in movies, but in real life, humans like to know when that kind of question is coming. Couples often talk this out, just so they know they're on the same page—and that they'll get a yes. You guys have discussed the basic terms of the engagement, and you're saving for a ring together. Proposing to him would be ignoring the plan, right?

If you don't want a big proposal—or a proposal at all—you have to let him know. Talk about it as a couple. That's what respectful partners do.

—Meredith

READERS? WHAT DO YOU THINK?

If you don't want a big ring or a big wedding, yet he is saving up for this before you two move forward, then I don't think you're on the same page as much as you think you are. — DORA79

Actually agree with Meredith on this one. It's not so much about gender roles as the fact that you'd be ignoring what he's told you. Not a good way to start. — HIDE THE SILVER

Listen to your heart and your gut, which are both on the same page. Propose to your boyfriend. Prove to him the "rock" doesn't matter. — OUTDOORCHICK

If my girlfriend proposed, I would say yes—but I'm not sure how my wife would feel about that. — RICH1273

Chapter 14

Dad

The advice column was about romance, not parenting, but one topic often involved the other.

Some letters written by single parents made me furious, especially when they reminded me of what I thought my own parents did wrong.

My mom involved me too much, even if I liked knowing (and advising her on) the details. My dad went the other way and didn't consider my opinion at all.

I hadn't communicated with my dad in years when I saw him at my sister's wedding. We were both in the ceremony; Ben's three sisters and I would be holding up the four poles of the huppah, and my mom and dad would walk Brette down the "aisle" on the beach in Wellfleet.

Brette had maintained a stronger bond with my dad over the years—they'd always shared a sense of humor—but she understood why I needed boundaries with him. She promised she'd seat us on opposite sides of the reception to avoid unnecessary contact. It was a gift.

"When's your dad getting here?" my mom asked, in the passenger seat of my car, as we waited for everyone else in the wedding party to arrive.

She wore a beautiful, shimmering white jacket. It had a high neck and matching pants—the black-tie version of a Hillary Clinton suit. She also wore a matching ivory hat to cover her head, which was mostly bald now. All that was left were wisps of brown-and-gray curls that made me think of baby birds.

She'd silently accepted that the hair loss wouldn't be minimal. I'd also noticed that she no longer brought up dating.

I considered my mom's question.

"Um, what do you mean 'When is Dad getting here?'" I asked.

"I mean, shouldn't he be here by now? It's time to get going. He's late."

I was confused by my mom's question because my father was standing in front of my car—like, right in front of us. His body was almost touching the hood, his eyes fixed on something far away, either because he was really looking at something in the distance or because he wanted to avoid eye contact with his ex-wife and estranged daughter. My mom hadn't seen him in more than a decade.

"Um, Mom, Dad's *right there*," I said.

"Where?"

"Like, literally in front of this vehicle."

I pointed to my dad.

My mom looked at the man in front of the car.

"No. That can't be him," she said, and then squinted, leaning forward. "Oh *God*. He looks so...old."

Then we both started laughing, and I watched my mom relax. I could tell it made her feel better that he'd lost some hair, too.

The wedding ceremony was beautiful and brief. Ben's cousins, a musical crew of hippie siblings, sang "Shining Star" by the Manhattans as my sister walked toward the huppah, one hand in my mother's, the other in my dad's. It was the first time in my adult life that I'd seen my mom and dad smiling about the same thing.

The guests in the rows of folding chairs on the beach were an eclectic mix of Ben's glassblowing community and Brette's friends, some of whom are actors, so they looked like people who would play wedding guests in a movie.

I saw Ben's friend Katya in person for the first time. She looked nice—not at all like someone who was conspiring to break up the relationship. She was smiling.

Mark, my date, was also in a seat, his eyes covered in dark shades. I could see him grinning as Ben went full millennial and read his vows off his cell phone.

I thought I could avoid seeing my dad after the ceremony—our seats felt miles apart—but I'd forgotten about the father-daughter dance. I had to watch as he and my sister swayed to that Israel Kamakawiwoʻole ukulele version of "Somewhere Over the Rainbow" and found myself fantasizing about cutting in.

"You haven't earned this!" I imagined shouting, as people gasped or maybe applauded.

But it was just child-of-divorce fan fiction in my head. In real life, I kept my arms at my sides, letting them enjoy the moment. My mom kept a neutral face.

After dinner, when the guests joined Brette and Ben on the dance floor, I began to set up the cotton candy machine.

Worth mentioning: I own an $800 cotton candy machine.

Shortly after I turned thirty, my mom asked me what I needed to be happy.

"A cotton candy machine," I answered, because I believed it was true.

As a kid, I'd decided that avoiding marriage and children would afford me the opportunity to live like Tom Hanks in *Big*, in an apartment filled with things like pinball machines, video games, and, most importantly, cotton candy.

I'd never let go of the plan, and as soon as I turned twenty-nine, I began getting estimates on machines—even talking to vendors at Fenway Park about buying something used.

At the time, though, there was no urgency because I was still dating Patrick, and he often brought me cotton candy after he went to a sporting event, presenting it like it was a bouquet of flowers.

But after we broke up, I had no cotton candy.

I wanted to be an independent woman and get my own.

"Can you afford a machine right now?" my mom had asked.

"No," I said. "Not really."

"What if I helped?" she asked.

It didn't seem right to take her money, but then I realized that if I never got married or had kids, she'd be spared those gift expenses. The machine *was* my wedding. She sent me a check for a few hundred bucks, and with what I'd already saved, I wound up finding a lightly used machine in Meredith, New Hampshire, of all places.

After that, I became the "cotton candy lady." I made it for Mark's kids, and offered to spin at the weddings of family and friends.

As I brought out the big silver apparatus for Brette's affair, some boy who looked about ten years old, a relative of Ben's, recognized what the machine was for and ran to my side.

There's always one kid at a formal event who wants to be the assistant cotton candy maker. He's usually the loner, or the one trying to avoid his relatives.

This kid was my guy. I'd seen him make a few bored faces at the start of the reception, but now, he had a purpose. We'd do this together.

As I handed him the box of cones, I felt a shadow approach. It was my dad.

Mark once asked me what my dad looked like, and I told him that he sort of resembled Harry, from *When Harry Met Sally*, in that first scene, when they meet at college. My dad looks like a nice short-ish guy who means no harm, and that's what he's always been. He's no villain.

"I want to talk to you," my dad said, as I balanced the silver cotton candy bowl on top of the machine base, not looking up. He appeared to be on a mission, ready to give a speech before I could walk away, no matter who was watching.

He took a breath and continued, his shoulders back, his face determined. "I know we don't speak much, and I know that's my fault. But I want a relationship with you. I want to know you, and I hope you'll let me be in your life in some way. That's all I want. I miss talking to you."

The words were lovely—but they weren't his. I could tell that my aunt Nancy and cousin Tina had thought up this monologue for my dad at their reception table. He'd even delivered the speech with Aunt Nancy's schoolteacher lilt.

My young assistant looked at me, his eyes asking, "Do we trust this guy?"

"I don't know," I said with a glance in return.

I watched my dad fidget, wondering what he really wanted. Would he have approached me at all if my aunt Nancy hadn't urged him to? His attempts to see me over the years were either the requirement of a divorce agreement or brought on by a lecture from a disappointed relative.

His most consistent trait was not showing up at all.

"Dad, what do you really want? Specifically?"

My dad paused and then shrugged. He'd run out of material.

"I'd like to be in touch, I guess," he said. "I'd like to check in once a week or so and see how you're doing."

It wasn't a crazy request. My young cotton candy friend's eyes met mine again, wondering how I might answer.

"I am so tired of this," my expression said in return.

My dad was never a mean person. He'd always been passive, almost overwhelmingly nice.

He moved to New Jersey when I was about nine or ten, just before my parents were officially divorced, to set up a life for himself on his own. I don't remember getting a specific cause of death for their marriage, but I knew my parents fought about money. I knew my mother didn't want him to drink.

One time, when I was really little, I remember finding him on the couch with a gash on his forehead. His face was pale, his eyes were closed, and I was petrified because I thought he was dead.

But it turned out he'd drunk too much at a party, fallen down, and then passed out. Later he'd claim he was dehydrated.

After my dad moved out, life got more comfortable in Maryland. The house felt less tense during the week, but when he visited us on the weekends, still sleeping on the couch, my mom looked frazzled.

Then, after what felt like a minute, he was living with another woman in New Jersey. I was ordered to take the train to see them twice a month, sometimes with Brette, sometimes alone.

My dad's new girlfriend was older than my mom. She was also tall and Nordic-looking, as if my dad had sought out the exact opposite of the woman he'd married. The girlfriend cooked a lot and always wanted to tell me what ingredients went into each dish.

Parsnips. Oregano. A little bit of Parmesan. Parsnips again. (To this day, Jess refers to her as "Parsnips.")

At Christmas, she decorated their home so extravagantly—with multiple trees, and a red-and-green stocking with my name on it—that I felt like a Hanukkah spirit was going to strike me down with a giant dreidel.

She and my dad filled their house with pets I was allergic to—the kind of cats that could send me to the hospital. I was always walking around a little bit dizzy and wheezing, afraid to sit on fabric chairs, wondering why my father hadn't said, "Hey, we can't get these pets if we want Meredith, my daughter, to be able to breathe."

Even this woman's slip-on shoes had little tigers on them. It made me feel like I was allergic to her, too.

They didn't tell me important things about their relationship, so I'd find out big news from other people. My grandmother was the one who told me they were dating. I learned they were engaged because I saw a congratulations card propped up on their television set. My father kept his head down as he confirmed their plans.

They didn't wait long to get married.

My stepmother was more open to drinking than my mother, and by the end of dinners at my dad's, they were often very drunk, in front of me. They were jolly about it, but sometimes they scared me and made me want to hide in my room.

Also, they seemed at ease with money when my mom wasn't. They had a motor boat and bought a house with a tennis court, while my mom didn't seem to have any disposable income at all. At home in Maryland, I'd find little pieces of paper with equations written all over them, my mother's quick attempts to figure out if we had enough to cover our monthly expenses.

My stepmother was nice enough, most of the time, but she was also always *there*, and seemed unwilling to give me any alone time with my father. After Brette went to college and I was old enough to decline weekend visits, I often opted to stay at home. I saw my dad a few times a year after turning eighteen, but I never went to his place by myself; I always brought a boyfriend or a friend because I felt I needed support.

Sometimes I would ask Draco to come and keep my stepmother busy so I could have ten minutes alone with my dad, just to see what it was like. It was difficult to pull off, but we'd strategize. Draco would ask her how she made the chicken parm, and then I'd be quick and say, "Hey, Dad, want to take a walk?"

If it worked, the walk was often disappointing. We remained silent or engaged in the worst small talk, and he didn't ask questions. He would bring his dog, Gus—the hairiest, most allergen-packed pet I could imagine—and I was sure I was the third wheel.

After college, all of the visits dried up. There were fights, one about an email forward he sent me that criticized Hillary Clinton, who at that time was a senator.

Some disagreements were about my stepmother. He knew I didn't like her.

"She is one of the kindest people I know," my dad would say. "Everyone thinks she is the *kindest person they know*."

She *was* kind in many ways. She taught me how to crochet when I was about fourteen, and when I moved into my first adult apartment, she bought me towels with pretty fish on them (sometimes she branched out from cats).

But nothing was on my terms. I didn't know how to make him understand that, as his kid, my comfort was supposed to come first, and that my father was supposed to want to spend time with me without his wife's supervision.

It wasn't as though my mom's choice of partners had thrilled me over the years. Sometimes she lost herself in her relationships, and I had to sit through tense dinners, listening to some guy talk about himself for hours.

Sometimes I was desperate for her to break up with a guy, knowing she deserved better.

But I knew she and I defined home in the same way. I grew up confident that no matter who my mom was with or where she took me, we'd end the night watching television together, or sitting at the kitchen table splitting an entire loaf of sourdough bread.

My dad and I never ended a night on the same team, and soon enough, as I entered my mid-twenties, our already infrequent calls dried up. He'd leave a voicemail on my birthday, but I wouldn't return it. Then those calls stopped, too.

One night, while I was still living with Jess, Brette called to tell me my dad had been diagnosed with colon cancer. This was years before my mom's diagnosis. His was caught at an earlier stage.

I remember saying to Brette, "That's the very treatable cancer, right? All men get that. He'll be fine."

"You're thinking of prostate cancer," Brette said.

"Oh."

He had surgery and a year of treatment, and I didn't call or email him once. Not after the diagnosis. Not during his year of hospital visits. Brette gave me updates, and it was like I was hearing about a distant friend of the family. I told her I wished him the best.

At the time, my mom asked whether I felt any guilt about not offering my support, and I assured her I didn't. It was the truth. He wouldn't have been there for me.

Now, at the wedding, I took a good look at him. He was so much older; we'd already missed so much. I couldn't imagine what we'd say to each other during once-a-week phone calls.

"I'm taking care of Mom, and you have your own life," I said, looking away. "Let's just focus on that."

My dad stood there, unscripted. Disappointed. I wanted him to walk away, but he just kept standing.

I looked down at my assistant, who'd lost interest in the adult drama, impatient to begin making the cotton candy.

Then I turned to my right and saw Mark. He'd appeared out of nowhere, sort of like Batman, standing behind me, his eyes glassy and his shoulders squared and confident from wedding booze.

More self-possessed than I'd ever seen him, Mark looked in the direction of my father, almost through him, and said, in a Batman voice, "I think we're done here."

My dad about-faced and went back to his table.

I was overcome by the strange mix of sadness and relief that I'd felt for more than thirty years every time I watched him walk away. I never knew what to do when my dad was around, but it didn't feel right when he was gone.

"Did I do the right thing?" Mark asked, now sounding less like Batman and more like Robin. "I didn't know what to do, but you looked uncomfortable so I stepped in…"

"That was the right thing," I assured him. "Thank you."

I got the cotton candy machine going, and before I knew it, there was a line for my services. My assistant handed me cone after cone.

In the distance, I could see Brette gyrating on the dance floor in her hot pink wedding dress. Nearby, my mom watched, her face radiating pure joy.

I am not an expert on parenting—other people write those columns—but there are a few things I'm sure about.

I know that divorces and family breakups are often necessary, and that you can't stay in a toxic relationship for "the sake of the children." But no matter what happens, kids should feel wanted and protected. Always. They shouldn't have to sit up at night worried about their dad's drinking. They shouldn't have to feel like a third wheel.

Letter writers who put their love lives before the kids feel the wrath—from me, and, more importantly, from the readers. Sometimes I feel bad when they're met with an angry mob, but mostly I just watch and read, sipping my coffee as the commenters pile on.

IS IT TIME TO END MY MARRIAGE?

Q. I'm thirty-one and I've been married for a few years, but I've been with my wife for eight. In the past I've wondered if maybe I only stayed with her so long because I didn't want to hurt her and I was too polite to end it. We have a toddler and one on the way.

The last year or so has been a challenge. I think we are both lonely, but I recognize it more than I feel like she does. Sometimes we fight, but the fights never get resolved. Each of us just avoids the other and then we don't talk until the next day, or whenever. I've been contemplating asking her for therapy, but I'm not sure it's worth it. We don't really have much in common, and we don't have much to talk about. When I talk she mostly ignores the things I tell her, and when she talks I get bored. Sex rarely occurs, and it's mostly if I persist. I'm thinking maybe we should split up before the kids get older and it becomes harder, but I can't bear the thought of not seeing my son every day, and I cry thinking about him missing me and me missing him. Is that a reason for us to stay together, unhappy?

To make matters worse, I can't stop thinking about a single coworker. We have a lot in common and we enjoy each other's company. I don't know if she feels any kind of way about me or not, and I can't plan to leave one woman just to go after another. I just need advice. Do I tell the other girl how I feel? Do I tell my wife about the other girl? Do I separate to try it out?

—Please Help!

♥

A. Somehow I knew paragraph three was coming. There's always a paragraph three with this kind of letter.

I understand that you have a big crush on this coworker, but she's not part of the equation right now. You want me to endorse the end of an eight-year relationship because you have the hots for someone at work, but I can't do that. Sorry.

Therapy is very worth it, because it'll give you the chance to talk about what's missing in your marriage. Starting a family and dealing with young kids can be hard on a partnership. There's little time and energy to focus on why you got together to begin with.

The good thing about the coworker is that she's made your needs clear. You miss conversation and interest. You miss shared experiences. Take that information to therapy with your wife. Put in some effort.

—Meredith

READERS? WHAT DO YOU THINK?

What makes therapy not worth it? Your kids aren't worth it? Happiness isn't worth it? What *is* worth it?

– SUREGONNAKNOWWEWEREHERE

Love it when a guy has a toddler, another on the way, and is still dreaming about some stranger and bolting to get it. "Take time to be a Dad today." And knock off the "crying" over missing your son. Just do the right thing and take care of your family. — STAUGUSTINE

When your son looks you in the face and says, "Daddy, why are you leaving us," are you going to have to say "I was too bored and lazy to try therapy?" If only to be able to say you did everything you could. — HIDE THE SILVER

You're an adult. You're married. You have one child and another on the way. You're not supposed to be happy right now, contrary to what you apparently believe. This is supposed to be tough, and before you throw away everything for the fantasy of something new, you need to work on your marriage. Stop asking what you're getting and start giving. — JUSTANOTHERBOSTONIAN

"Stop asking what you're getting and start giving." This. I'm going to have this embroidered on a sampler. — ENJOYEVERYSANDWICH

What makes you think your unhappily married, father-to-be status is even remotely appealing to a single coworker? You, sir, are a tool. — MARIENNA

Chapter 15

Grilled Cheese

Sometimes when you're busy writing a love advice column and trying to help your mother accept that she'll spend the rest of her life on chemotherapy, you neglect to have intercourse. For years.

You forget that sex is a thing that you're supposed to want to do. Even when you have dates with nice people—some of whom take you to that tapas place in the South End with the really good corn with the cotija cheese on it—getting naked with them seems strange, and like it'd be a crazy hassle, so you just go home.

You know this isn't normal, so you're worried. You wonder if you will ever have sex again.

You begin to resent acquaintances who tell you that this is just a lull, because when you google "lull" it's defined as "temporary interval" or "breather," and that is not what this is.

Whatever your vagina is doing, it is the opposite of breathing.

You also resent your friends because they seem to have sex—and to enjoy it—without much effort. The Rachels, who are young enough to have had the HPV vaccine, talk about having sex like it's as easy as blinking. As easy as Snapchat. They have effortless orgasms. Everything happens in an instant.

"You should do Tinder," they say.

It's a new app, and you have seen them use it, but it looks like your version of hell. Men on Tinder choose pictures of themselves from weddings that show them standing next to eight other similar-looking guys in suits, all with beers in their hands. You can't figure out how the Rachels can tell which guy they're judging for the swipe.

Every time you say the word "swipe," you lose a little bit of hope that you'll ever experience physical intimacy again.

Meanwhile, your married friends, who you thought might be bored of sex by now, are apparently on top of each other all the time. Mark, for instance, who has been with Michelle for more than twenty years, tells you that they've been having sex a lot. They are having some sort of sexual renaissance. It's fantastic.

The more you hear stories about people you know having sex, the less you understand the concept. The idea of two people touching tongues—sometimes without brushing their teeth first!—seems crazy; you're pretty sure you get more than enough germs when you're with your mom at Mass General.

Your breasts, which you used to believe were the most attractive things on your body, have become weights that inhibit you from doing anything above Level 4 on the elliptical machine at Planet Fitness. Your periods make you want to stomp on a city. Your knees hurt. You ask your doctor whether you might be premenopausal in your mid-thirties, but she rolls her eyes and tells you it's probably stress. She asks you whether you've tried Jdate.

You can't believe you ever even *kissed* Patrick. When you run into him in the *Globe* cafeteria and remember that you used to be attracted to him, you are confused. What was that like? How did your brain even work that way? It's all so baffling.

Even your special brand of pornography doesn't help. The images of vampires that used to inspire masturbatory feats now calm you like Valium. Instead of picturing Edward Cullen twisting you into a flexible pretzel and breaking the skin on your neck with his teeth, you imagine *eating* a soft pretzel with him on the couch while you watch *Parks and Recreation*.

You imagine him fully clothed. You wonder what he'd think of Ron Swanson.

"That Ron Swanson," Edward Cullen would say. "He *really* hates technology."

Meanwhile, because you are an advice columnist, people write to you with questions about sex.

Specifically, they want to know why sex—or the lack thereof—is making them miserable.

You feel like a certifiable fraud answering these letters, because you have to pretend you understand that sex can be nice and fun. You have to convince readers that you understand why they want it.

In some ways, you find it comforting that many letter writers are going without.

Straight women, in particular, who were told at a young

age that men think about sex every ten seconds, write in to say they feel rejected because their boyfriends and husbands don't want it as much as they do. It makes them feel ugly and awful, and they wonder what they're doing wrong.

You do your best to help these women, even though you empathize with their partners.

You are grateful that you don't have to reject anyone right now.

You think about the most popular letter from your column—which ran during your first year on the job. A man had written in explaining that his longtime girlfriend refused to give him oral sex. He wanted to marry her, but couldn't imagine living the rest of his life without blow jobs. The idea was devastating.

You weren't allowed to say "blow job" on the *Boston Globe*'s website, so you told readers you were using a euphemism. It happened to be what you were eating for lunch: "grilled cheese."

Every time he wrote the phrase "blow job," you replaced it with "grilled cheese sandwiches" in brackets.

"The thought of going the rest of my life without receiving [grilled cheese sandwiches] is definitely a worry," the letter writer stated, with your edits. "I fear I may resent her eventually, or possibly feel the need to seek [grilled cheese sandwiches] out somewhere else when enough time has passed."

Even though you and readers suspected that the letter was a prank—maybe from someone testing to see whether you'd post that kind of problem on your site—you answered with empathy. You told the letter writer that a relationship can't be good if you're always longing for grilled cheese. You told him to find someone who *wants* to make it.

Now, though, you can't imagine grilled cheese ever being a priority. Maybe because your mom lives down the street and she is probably calling you *right now*.

The letter writers you relate to most are the insecure, self-proclaimed virgins, and as it turns out, there are many of them. Every few months you hear from a person in their twenties, or older, who has never gone "all the way."

One writer in particular is worried about how she'll tell her first partner about her inexperience. She has started dating someone she likes, but will he run if he knows?

"Is this a secret I should bury?" she asks.

You empathize, because it's starting to feel like you have a shameful secret of your own, even when you're with your friends.

You get quiet when they talk about their own sex lives. Some say they haven't gotten laid in months. A *year*. This is tragic to them. Then they look at you and remember who they're talking to.

You do the math:

Rihanna has put out four albums since you last had sex.
It has snowed more than 80 inches in Boston since you last had sex.
David Ortiz has hit 135 home runs since you last had sex.
Tom Cruise and Katie Holmes were still married the last time you had sex.

You decide to tell these inexperienced letter writers that even though the people they date may have more experience, "they've never had sex with you," so, to some extent, everyone is a beginner.

You are by no means a sex columnist, but you know you must tell people to broaden how they define sex, because it's not all about penises penetrating holes. Defining virginity and sexual experience in such narrow terms doesn't help anybody.

You try to persuade readers who are experiencing a lull that "not using it" does not mean "losing it," and that there is no shame in taking a break.

Then you remind yourself that deep down, you believe your own advice. If it is true for others, it's true for you.

You look at the picture of Robert Pattinson on your refrigerator and he seems to agree.

HER SEX DRIVE OUTPACES HIS

Q. My boyfriend and I are in our mid-to-late twenties, have been dating for two years, and are really happy together. We love each other's families, we don't bicker or fight very often, we laugh all the time, and we can definitely see a future together.

We don't live together yet, but we've talked about it since I do spend most nights at his place anyway. The problem I'm having seems to be the opposite of most other relationships—I have a MUCH higher sex drive than him, and am constantly getting turned down for sex by him. When we do have sex, it's amazing; it's just not nearly as frequent as I'd like. Since I know readers will be curious/want context, it's currently one to two times a week, and while I'd love daily, I'd be happy with three to four times a week. The first year we were dating (I know, I know, the honeymoon phase), we seemed to be more on the same page, but now our needs seem to have gotten farther apart. I've always heard that women's sexual peak is in their thirties while men hit theirs in their early twenties. If this is the case, I'm worried I'll become even more unsatisfied in an important area of our relationship as I want it even more and he wants it even less.

My ex-boyfriend was pretty sex-crazed and ended up cheating on me, so I'm trying to see a lower sex drive as a positive thing, especially since my current relationship is the best one I've ever been in. Is there a way to compromise or to get him more interested? Or is our sex life going to be totally doomed further down the road?

—Sexually Frustrated

A. You're not doomed. Really, if I'm doing the math right, you'd be happy with one more night (or morning) of sex each week. Maybe two. That's not a big jump.

What concerns me is how you're both dealing with the issue. Constant sexual rejection can kill a relationship. You need to talk to your boyfriend about your desires and find out if there's a way to have more sex without it feeling like an obligation. Find out when he likes sex most. Ask him what he enjoys, in general. Maybe you should be initiating it at a different time of day…or trying something new.

Have the conversation when you're both relaxed and in a good mood. Let him know this isn't a judgment—it's just something that should be discussed before there's a move-in. Know that it doesn't have to be a very serious talk. If you're the kind of couple that laughs a lot, you can have fun with this.

Also know that this isn't "the opposite of most other relationships." The whole "men always want to have sex" thing is a myth. Some men do, some men don't. There are many women out there who want more.

—Meredith

READERS? WHAT DO YOU THINK?

I feel your pain. I have the same problem. Women I date have zero interest in sex and it is a relationship killer. I won't sugarcoat it. I agree with Meredith. Talk to your boyfriend about it without judgment. Sometimes it comes down to changing routines, maybe getting a bit more creative, whatever. You won't know unless you ask him about it, but don't make it an all or nothing. It sounds like the rest of your relationship is great so keep that in mind when you discuss this with him. Best of luck. — PATSFAN70

My ex would never do it at normal hours, I had to wake him up at the weirdest hours. 3 to 4 a.m. were peak…not sure if this is normal. I'd do it with a cup of coffee in hand. — LEESYWEESY

If it's not on fire in your twenties—early in the relationship—bail. Nicely, but bail. — SUPERCHICK

ALLERGIC TO GRILLED CHEESE

Q. I am a thirty-year-old male. I have been dating a wonderful woman for 2.5 years. I would describe everything about her as perfect except for one thing:

She absolutely refuses to [make me a grilled cheese sandwich].

Now I want to ask her to marry me, but the thought of going the rest of my life without receiving [grilled cheese sandwiches] is definitely a worry. I fear I may resent her eventually, or possibly feel the need to seek [grilled cheese sandwiches] out somewhere else when enough time has passed.

It has already been 2.5+ years since I last experienced a [grilled cheese sandwich]. It is starting to consume my thoughts. I don't know if this one thing is enough to be a deal breaker. Everything else is perfect. I don't know what to do!

—[Needing Grilled Cheese], Boston

A. Have you talked to this woman about why she's so opposed to grilled cheese? Do her reasons seem valid and specific (past trauma, health issues, etc.)? Is there any room for negotiation? Has she always been opposed to grilled cheese or is it just specific to you?

You must tell her that the lack of grilled cheese is standing in the way of your commitment. I know it's difficult to say—it sounds so petty and selfish—but I'm here to tell you it's a valid concern. You've probably heard this before, but disagreements about sex and money are usually what end relationships. If you're resenting her now, fast-forward ten years. It will get worse.

Grilled cheese sandwiches are awesome. Especially with tomatoes and fancy cheese, like Brie. But some people would rather eat them than make them. And some people are allergic to them and can't go near them.

But you're not allergic. You like them a lot. If your girlfriend can't come up with a grilled cheese compromise, then yes, this may be a deal breaker. Ask yourself: Is the rest of her perfect enough to balance the sexual incompatibility?

—Meredith

READERS? WHAT DO YOU THINK?

I absolutely detest making grilled cheese. My husband enjoys it, so from time to time, I put his needs first and make him the best darn grilled cheese I can—no halfhearted *are we there yet* cooking. One factor of any successful relationship is that each party is willing to put their partner's needs ahead of their own sometimes. — AKMOM

It would be REALLY helpful to know WHY she refuses to make grilled cheese sandwiches. Do you talk about this all the time or constantly ask for it? If you do, that's annoying and could possibly cause her to NOT want to do it even more. — GRILLEDCHEESEEXPERT

Do you make grilled cheese for her? If not, you can't really get upset if she doesn't make you any. — MCHZ

There are plenty of ladies who love making the grilled cheese. Find one. And make as many grilled cheese sandwiches as possible. In the car. Taking a shower. Trying on

some new swim trunks. Jury duty. Christmas shopping...And then pay back the love of course.
— BJAMIN1884

One thing you can do is start by making a Triscuit with a little melted cheese on top. These are easy to make and yummy to eat—indeed, bite-size food is all the rage these days (amuse bouche is the correct culinary term, right?). Later, you can graduate to half sandwiches and have fun with those until she's ready to make a whole one. Also, make sure that when you graduate to the whole sandwich, she's well aware of how fast or slow it takes for you to finish it. — MISCREATION

Chapter 16

Yo-Yo Ma

I never thought I was the kind of person who would write in to an advice column.

Even before I'd started writing *Love Letters*, I'd never been tempted.

It's not that I thought I was better than anyone else; I was just scared to write it all down. I was too afraid to be public, even under a fake name.

But sometimes you're so desperate for an answer to a question—so in need of comfort—that you'll reach out to anyone who will listen, whether it's in real life or online.

I found myself in that place in May of 2013.

It had been an easy few weeks. The weather had been nice, which made it easier for my mom to go outside. Mark and I had taken her to see *The Book of Mormon*. We got really good seats.

She seemed really happy and said Boston officially felt like home.

But about a week later, she complained that she was feeling

a little sick and run-down. It didn't seem urgent to me, but Brette came up to visit and assist.

Once she arrived, she made a quick assessment.

"I don't like this," Brette said from my mom's apartment. "She has a fever. I think I'm going to bring her to the hospital."

"Shit. Do we have to?" I asked. "You know everyone at the hospital is sick. If we bring her in, we risk her getting even sicker."

"I have a bad feeling and I think we should go," Brette said.

They headed over to Mass General. Hours later, Brette called to tell me our mom had been admitted.

"Fuck," I said, annoyed that the next few days of work might be shot.

It was a weekend, which meant our regular oncologist wasn't around. We were in an overnight room in Mass General's main building, and they were pumping her with antibiotics trying to tame her fever, which kept spiking and we didn't know why.

I snapped at the doctor because he looked like a teenager.

"So what is the plan?" I asked.

I just wanted all of us to be able to go home.

"Antibiotics should control the fever," the doctor said. "Hopefully we'll bring the temperature down soon."

We were there another day, and the fever persisted. My mom started crying a little because she was frustrated, desperate to get out of there.

"What do you need?" Brette asked.

"I just want to go home," she said.

"You can't go home right now," I said, my tone harsh.

The IVs of antibiotics—there were a few of them—were scaring me. The nurses gave us uncomfortable looks. They weren't upbeat like the nurses on the chemo floor, who knew us by name and remembered little details about our lives.

"I wish..." my mom said, in her youngest-sounding voice, "I wish that Yo-Yo Ma would come to my hospital room and play for me."

I wasn't in the mood for her helpless princess voice.

Plus, asking to hear music in a hospital room felt like the thing one does before one dies. It felt like a last request, and it freaked me out.

"I'm pretty sure Yo-Yo Ma is a real dick," I said.

I spat out the words, exasperation clouding my tone.

For the record, I have no idea whether Yo-Yo Ma is a dick. He lives around Boston, and on the occasions I've run into him at events covered by the *Globe*, he hasn't seemed like a dick at all. If anything, he's appeared to be generous and lovely, always happy to volunteer his time and talent for good causes. One time I saw him in a hotel in Harvard Square being nice to staff members, smiling like he was the kindest guy on the planet.

I only said Yo-Yo Ma was a dick because I was stressed and tired, and because sometimes when you're frightened, you say shitty things, even to your mother in an emergency room.

As the words "Yo-Yo Ma is a real dick" left my mouth, my mother went silent. Her jaw dropped, almost in slow motion.

Had I renounced God in that hospital room, my mother wouldn't have cared. But one *did not* blaspheme Yo-Yo Ma. One did not call the leader of the Silk Road Ensemble the D-word.

My mother looked away, horrified by her child.

"My leg hurts," she mumbled.

"Did you pull a muscle or something on the treadmill?" Brette asked.

"Maybe," my mom said. "It feels like a cramp or a bruise."

We sat there for hours, watching the liquid drip through tubes connected to her hands, until Brette decided it was time to "re-cast." It was a casting director strategy she liked to apply to real life; sometimes you just need to re-cast the scene. This team of hospital staffers weren't getting it done, so it was time to bring in an understudy.

"What if we called palliative care?" she asked.

"Is this the kind of thing they'd help with?" I responded.

"Palliative care people are about quality of life. They're advocates, and right now, we need a fucking advocate. We need someone to tell us what to do if the fever doesn't go down."

The hospital paged the palliative care nurse on call, who arrived within an hour.

And that's when I met him. Sebastian.

He wore a suit shirt and khaki pants, and his beard looked soft and bristly at the same time—the kind of beard that would tickle you while kissing. He seemed about my age, maybe younger. He was my preferred height, not too tall—maybe 5'9"—which meant I could look into his eyes. For the first time in my life, I thought to look for a ring on a man's finger. I didn't see one.

I wasn't the only one who'd looked. My mom's face went from miserable to flirtatious, and she smiled like she wasn't sick anymore and would be available for a date later that night.

"What seems to be the problem?" Sebastian asked, and I wanted to yell "Everything!" and then ask him to hold me. I tried to find anything in the room that was reflective to check my hair. I ran my tongue over my teeth, checking for stray food.

Sebastian sat on the edge of my mom's hospital bed and asked her about her pain. He touched her leg. "It hurts right there?"

"Yes," she murmured. "Right there."

"Could it be a pulled muscle?" I asked, wanting to remind Sebastian that I was in the room, age-appropriate, and also unmarried. I tried to breathe only out of my nose, because I knew my breath smelled like garlic naan.

"It could be, but we'll make sure it gets checked out," Sebastian said.

Seconds after he left the room, promising to return to check in on us, we erupted.

"Holy shit," Brette said.

"Wow," my mom said.

"Sebastian," I said to myself, believing in meet-cutes for the first time.

I imagined our future.

Sebastian would return late from work, having helped sick people all day, because he is a kind person, and I'd be in front of my laptop, writing my column, or maybe a novel loosely based on our own love story. He'd have picked up takeout on the way home, and would be excited to hear about my day, and to share stories of how many lives he'd saved at Mass General.

We'd have low-effort-but-serviceable sex, barely awake, the kind you can have with someone who knows exactly what you like, someone you've already impressed.

We'd talk about my mom, who'd be living with us in our two-family home in Jamaica Plain, in walking distance to Vee Vee, the restaurant where we'd get oysters once a week.

"You guys go home," my mom said, interrupting my fantasy narrative.

"Right," I said. "We should all sleep."

I began to pack up for the night. Brette and I didn't sleep in hospitals because we found that with her Crohn's and my chronic asthma, we'd always wind up sick and unhelpful. We made a plan with the doctors to scan her leg in the morning, just in case. The nurses said they'd call if her fever got worse.

The call from the doctor came in at about five in the morning. He said he needed to intubate and wanted my permission.

"Wait, what?" I said, groggy as I jumped from my bed and ran to the couch to shake Brette, who'd had a few hours of fitful sleep on my couch. "Intubate?"

"Your mom had a bad night," the doctor said, "and then she lost consciousness. We need to intubate. You need to give me permission right now."

"Then do it!" I said.

We ran for my car, and then sped down the empty roads around Boston Common to get to Mass General's parking lot. By the time we were inside the building, she was in the ICU. Her skin was paper-white, the tube and mask obstructing much of her face. She looked like she was in some sort of coma.

Her leg had been scanned, and it showed an abscess. That was the source of the previous day's pain—it had been an infection.

"We're going to surgically remove the abscess, and then let her heal," the ICU doctor said. "Then hopefully she'll wake up, once her body gets strong again."

Everything was blurry.

"Wait, hopefully?" I asked, dazed.

Brette added a list of questions about next steps. I couldn't comprehend the answers.

Later, when my mom's oncologist stopped by, he looked relaxed and warm, which made me feel better. I emailed someone at work to press "publish" on my column.

I called Jess. I called Mark. I texted Patrick to say that my mom was unconscious in the hospital, and then regretted it. I didn't want him to feel pressured to comfort me, but I also thought he should know.

"I'll stop by," he replied.

Patrick drove over during his lunch break. We walked around Mass General's hallways, and he was mostly silent as I told him everything I knew, which was that post-surgery, we were waiting for my mom to open her eyes.

After a few loops around the floor, we were back where we started, in front of the ICU's double doors.

"Do you want to come see her? And Brette?"

He looked down at the painted line on the floor that separated the hallway from the intensive care rooms. Patrick shook his head no.

I nodded, understanding the boundary. He was a friend now—not the guy who could cross that line and be more.

"Thanks for coming," I said.

He answered with a loving shrug.

Later, Mark was there to make sure I got dinner. I explained to him that the abscess was gone, but no one could tell us how long the wake-up would take. Not too long, I hoped.

It was the oncologist who told me we were in trouble. He stopped by again, just as Mark and I were about to do a food run.

"She's very, very sick, Meredith," the oncologist said. "She might not wake up."

He looked as if he had shocked himself by saying it.

"But they removed the abscess," I said. "So the infection should go away, right? And then she wakes up?"

The oncologist repeated himself. "She's very sick."

"But it's *possible* she'll wake up, right?"

Brette was with me now, quiet.

"Yes, it's possible," the doctor said, trying to smile, as Mark stood nearby, attempting to mask the fear on his face. "Anything is possible right now."

Mark said we should eat something and pick up clothes, so we stopped for takeout and went back to my apartment. Brette stayed at the hospital with Aunt Nancy. I knew she was also probably calling my dad.

I was manic as I grabbed things from my bedroom, not knowing what I needed.

Mark dropped me back off at the hospital an hour or so later, telling me "good luck," because there was nothing else to say.

As the hours passed, the hospital started to remind me of a casino because I couldn't tell what time it was, and the air felt oxidized and impure. We didn't know what to do with ourselves, except for Ben, who got water, which was much appreciated because we were all dehydrated. I got a text from Mark's twelve-year-old daughter that said, "You are part of my family." I wept and wondered what Mark had told her.

I paced for a while and thought that if I were in a movie, my character would find the hospital chapel and say something dramatic, but in real life, I didn't want to do that. I just wanted to be close to Brette and my mom. I wanted to listen to the *shh*-ing noises from the machines that ensured that the antibiotics were still filtering down the tubes, into the IV.

Near midnight, I called my friend Paul's parents.

Paul Sr. was a retired hospital social worker, so he understood the language of ICUs, and Paul's mom was an expert comforter and had become a friend to my mother in Boston; I knew my mom would want her there.

There wasn't much for Paul's parents to do, though. Once they arrived, they were waiting around like the rest of us for something to change.

At about 2 a.m., I realized that I didn't have a *Love Letters* column set to run for the next day. I'd only been working two days ahead, so there was nothing in the queue.

I'd never not posted. My mom had always yelled, even from hospital rooms, "Did you post the letter yet? Make sure you post!"

But I couldn't choose a letter and come up with a solid answer in the middle of the night in the hospital. Not with my mother unconscious on machines.

I opened my laptop in one of the waiting rooms and grabbed a random letter from my inbox. I published it as a question without an answer, and explained to readers that I was dealing with a family emergency, and that they'd have to be the experts on their own.

At about 5 a.m., the doctor on rotation, a woman who looked young enough to be a Rachel, took us into a conference room with Paul's parents and Aunt Nancy, and asked if we were ready to let go.

This young doctor meant death. She meant that this stupid leg infection, which was a hiccup—a side effect—was going to make my mother disappear.

"You need to make a decision about resuscitation," the doctor said.

"There's no decision to be made," I said. "We'll resuscitate. Of course we'll resuscitate. My mom is not some old lady who wants to die."

"I don't think you understand," the doctor said.

"No, I understand perfectly," I said. "My mother wants to live, no matter what. Even if you have to cut off all of her body parts and we have to walk around with her as a talking head in a jar, she'll choose that over death. She'll want to live, no matter the cost."

The young doctor nodded—she was respectful—but then explained what I had missed, which was that at some point during the night, the magic post-coma wakeup had ceased to be an option. My beautiful mother, who had always been full of life and romance and first dates and music, would not pop up from her bed in the ICU, gasping for breath as she came to, like comatose people do on medical shows.

"Resuscitation," in this case, meant doing chest compressions as she coded. Cracking my mother's ribs as she flatlined. Giving her a few last moments of technical life before inevitable death.

"Then crack her chest," I said. "Keep her alive as long as possible."

Maybe cracking her chest would wake her up.

Brette stopped me there, our four-year age difference more pronounced than it had ever been. She looked at me with the eyes of a guardian.

"Meredith, I've read that people can perceive things that happen to them during the last moments of their life, even if they're unconscious. I don't want Mom's last memories to be the experience of someone breaking her chest in two. She's gone. We should let her go peacefully."

I looked at Paul Sr., and he nodded. Everyone nodded but me.

There's not much to do when you're waiting for somebody to die. My aunt Nancy paced. Ben stood nearby like a bearded bloodhound.

I was sitting in the waiting room when Brette came and

explained that I had to say goodbye. She said she had already given my mom her own official goodbye, and now it was my turn. It seemed like a worthless thing to do—to say last words to someone who couldn't hear them.

But Brette was sure my mom could hear everything.

The room was dark as I stood by the bed. The glowing lines on the machines reminded me of *Grey's Anatomy*, and I thought of that ferry-boat-crash arc of the show, where Meredith Grey almost drowns.

My mom and I made fun of that plotline because it was so dramatic. I remembered talking on the phone about it one night while I was at Patrick's apartment.

"Are you going to watch *Grey's*?" she asked.

"Of course. I mean, it's the FERRY BOAT DISASTER," I said, and she'd cracked up.

"That stupid boat," she responded.

I don't remember everything I told my mom in the hospital room. I know I reminded her of some weird things we did, and I know I said "thank you" a lot while I cried.

More than anything, in those moments, I felt gratitude. I felt so lucky to have known her so well.

After I had run out of words, I brought my laptop into the room and opened iTunes—because the Rachels had not yet taught me to use Spotify—and downloaded *The Essential Yo-Yo Ma*. I began to play the first song, a Bach cello suite, which I imagined she'd enjoy with her eyes closed, doing that dreamy head-swaying thing she did whenever she listened to musicians she adored.

From Yo-Yo Ma, I moved on to her other favorites—*our* favorites.

Sting's "The Hounds of Winter." She used to blast that one in our living room in Maryland while she was making dinner. We'd heard him play it live so many times. Now the lyrics were all for her.

"*It seems that she's gone, leaving me too soon.*"

She loved the English band Bombay Bicycle Club, having found them through the *Twilight* soundtracks. Her favorite of their songs was "Fairytale Lullaby," a cover, so I played it. The lyrics were about sugar fish that grant your every wish.

"*And if you want your friends to come, then bring them all along.*"

I'd never really listened to the lyrics, but they're what I heard in the end.

That's when she was at her happiest, when she was surrounded by her piano students, her daughters, her friends. That's when I was at my happiest, too, when I brought everyone along.

She died at about seven in the morning.

Then we stood in the hallway waiting for someone to tell us what to do next.

I was surprised I was hungry. I was desperate for a muffin.

Brette had the ICU nurses page Sebastian, who was already back at the hospital for his early shift. He was freshly showered and in a clean suit shirt. I had not brushed my teeth in two days and was surprised I cared.

He expressed condolences and gave us hugs. Then, after a

few minutes of standing there in silence, he politely told us that as a palliative care nurse, his job was done. He had to go tend to the living.

"I know. But I don't want you to go," Brette said. "Our mom just died, so can I touch your beard?"

"Sure," Sebastian told her, without flinching, like the request was normal. "Of course."

She rubbed it like it was a genie's lamp.

"Thanks for everything," I said, and he nodded.

I watched his khaki pants as he walked away. I wished *I* had touched his beard.

I would google Sebastian, I decided in that moment. Life was too short and I had nothing to lose.

They moved us to a conference room so we didn't upset other ICU patients while we talked about what to do with the body. The room had a big, round laminate table, and I was surprised to see that every seat was taken.

Brette, Ben, Aunt Nancy, my uncle Tim, Paul's parents, Mark, and Danielle, who, when it comes to support during tragedies, is the nucleus.

I found out from Danielle that she and Jess had been waiting in a restaurant across the street from the hospital as my mother was dying. I'd gone out of my way not to call Jess when it got bad—I was worried about her feeling obligated to leave the kids, and I didn't want her to have to experience this pain—but she had stayed close, just in case I needed her.

Babies or not, Jess would always be there for me, just as I would be for her. I should have known.

Details were discussed. Danielle offered to call funeral homes.

We drove back to my apartment and Mark started vacuuming my rug. The *Globe* gave him bereavement time, too.

Lasagna started coming like we had planted magic pasta seeds in the refrigerator. Paul's mom made a dessert I began referring to as "death cake," a mix of pineapple and sugary frosting.

Brette didn't want to eat. I ate everything.

I took a Klonopin that night and washed it down with wine. I passed out around two a.m. and woke up at seven, feeling like the previous day could have been a dream. But then I saw Brette and Ben tossing and turning on my couch, and their bags on the living room floor. It had all happened.

I figured I should start calling people, like my bosses and acquaintances and distant relatives. Maybe my mom's cousin Mimi, whom I'd never met, but I knew she lived in Connecticut. Or what about my mom's ex-fiancé, who'd never even been told she was sick? Were we supposed to call him?

It was a good question for an advice column.

Which reminded me of my mother's morning question. "Did you post your letter yet?"

I knew it would have been okay to skip the column that morning, but I didn't want to.

Before I opened my door to the family and friends, I wanted to talk to the people I wouldn't recognize on the street, but who'd kept me company for years.

Maybe I wanted to crowd-source my grief.

I didn't read the comments on the post for months, but I was happy knowing they'd be there when I was ready.

PLAY ME SOME MUSIC

I lost my mom yesterday. It was unexpected—sort of.

She was actually diagnosed with cancer about a year after I started *Love Letters*. The cancer wasn't what ended things. It was some weird, acute infection. Very random, very rare. Everyone at the hospital looked shocked because they thought she had many years ahead of her.

I'm oversharing a bit today because you letter writers are always so exposed in this column, and I get to be nice and private, for the most part. Four years ago, when my mom was diagnosed, we decided she'd move to Boston. She loved it here, and we tried to forget that cancer was one of her reasons for relocating.

During these years, I've had many *Love Letters* questions of my own. How can I be fun on a date when I'm anxious about my mom's health? Or yesterday, shortly after she died, was it safe to let ex-boyfriends show up to comfort me? Will their attention confuse me? Because my instinct was to want to stand next to them, remembering a different time when things were easier.

Maybe you have some advice for me. I don't know.

What I do know is that Jewish people sit shiva, which is basically a mourning period after death where you sit around. It's probably more complicated than that, but my immediate family isn't very observant.

Yesterday, when the doctors asked me if my mom was religious, I explained that she was a musician. She went to Juilliard, and concert halls were churches to her. (I know you all hate that I love the movie *Twilight*, but one of the reasons is that it got my mom's piano students excited about Debussy. Robert Pattinson listens to "Clair de Lune" in that movie, and all of a sudden my mom's young students were desperate to learn the piece. Mom called the film "piano teacher porn.")

My version of shiva involves sweatpants, food, and taking a day off from *Love Letters*, which entertained her so much, especially during boring cancer treatments. We'll be back to regular letters on Monday, but for today, I'd like you to do me a favor. My mom was a ridiculous romantic. She was weirdly incapable of cynicism when it comes to love, which earned her more than a few eye rolls from me. I'd love for you to use today's comments space to tell me a romantic story, post a link to a romantic song, or give me some advice about the questions I mentioned earlier. Thank you for assistance with shiva and all of this.

Now, if you don't mind, help.

—Meredith

If it wasn't for you, I never would have met Alice. And if I hadn't met Alice, I wouldn't have gone to New Orleans. If I hadn't gone to New Orleans, I wouldn't be getting married a week from today. Thanks for you, Meredith. You have my heart, too. — SALLY

Mine as well. You're in my thoughts, Meredith. — ALICE

I think at this time, whoever wants to console you, ex or not, just... let them. You're going through a tough time right now so I don't think normal rules apply. — GOLDIE31

When you're ready, play "So Happy Together" by the Turtles. As for ex-boyfriends—I'd say no, you're vulnerable and hurting. Look for support from your girlfriends and family; too easy to get confused with the exes. Be kind to you. — VCWRITER

Brahms Intermezzo Op 117/1; Schubert Impromptu Op 90/3. — STAUGUSTINE

Shiva? Isn't that what Natalie Merchant does just thinking about the weather? Hoping family, friends, and boys who used to pitch your woo are helping you along on this day. We are all sending our love your way. — VALENTINO

Meredith, one of the few irrational things I believe without question is that a mother who loves her daughter carries her in her soul wherever she goes, forever. From wherever she is now, she will make sure you are able to come to some peace of mind eventually, and she will continue to delight in your happiness and successes. — THE_BRIDE

Rico's feelings on Shiva is to not mourn your mom's life but to celebrate her life, remember those good times, the times she made you laugh, cry, roll your eyes... Rico wishes he knew your mom; Rico is a huge music fan himself and had a relative, also female (she'd be 100 or more if alive), who went to Juilliard as well... Rico hopes you have recordings of her playing... Piano is beautiful. — RICO

I've been lurking since *Love Letters* began. Meredith, my thoughts are with you and your family. I hope that the wonderful memories of your mother give you some comfort over the days and years ahead. May you always feel her presence in your heart and know that she is with you.
— SHEZ2013

I wrote in a few years ago after a particularly horrendous breakup. I had started dating someone I had known for years but was nowhere near healed from the trauma I'd been put through. Everyone here told me to let this great guy go if I didn't want to be with him because someone else would love to date him. I stayed. He was patient. We were both honest with each other. It worked out. It's been almost three and a half years. What started as long distance between NY and MA has resulted in my relocation to Yankee territory and we've been living and loving together for over a year now. While I didn't take the advice of you or the readers, two parts of that process really helped. It was incredibly enlightening to see my words written out and to directly compare the hurt that had been done by someone I was still clinging to with the gentle love, support, and laughter that was being offered by someone I hadn't really given a chance to. I was not being fair to him, someone that I had known for years and really cared about from the beginning, and your response and the readers' responses were the smack that I needed. So thank you, Meredith. For giving so much of yourself and facilitating the giving of others in this wonderful space. Your mother's legacy lives on in all of us who share her joy in reading *Love Letters* every day. — LABAMBS

My advice is to take comfort wherever it is offered.
— ENJOYEVERYSANDWICH

Chapter 17

IRL (One Year Later)

A year after my mom's death, I was on a plane flipping through my television options on a flight to Paris. The trip would be at least six hours, so there would be time to start *Game of Thrones*. The show was one of the many things I'd missed during the hectic years of her illness.

I felt warmth next to me, Sebastian's arm at my side. I turned to the left to find his big brown eyes fixed on mine, his expression a mix of love and excitement. After we made it across the Atlantic, we'd share a flat for a week in Europe. Our first big trip.

Except it wasn't really Sebastian. Not at all.

My college friend Brad, a nurse with connections at Mass General, had done some digging around about Sebastian for me, and discovered that my mom's smoking-hot palliative care nurse was gay, so that was that.

In reality, the man at my side was Mark, and he wasn't looking at me with love. His eyes were wide and goofy because he'd just figured out that he didn't have to pay for whiskey on the plane.

"Free booze on international flights!" he said. "Free!"

Before I could respond, he cued up an episode of *Veep*.

On my right was my aunt Nancy. She'd already started an episode of *Thrones* on the small screen in front of her seat and kept turning her head to avoid the violence.

"I can't look," she said, giggling as she squinted to avoid seeing a young Stark child get pushed out of a window.

We were at the start of what would be a family trip for the four of us; Brette was on her own flight from New York City and would meet us in Paris, where we planned to mark the first anniversary of my mom's death.

It was a strange group—no spouses, just Brette, Aunt Nancy, Mark, and me—but to my mother, it would have made perfect sense.

I'd already cued up *Love Letters* to post from abroad. The usual topics were represented: "She Doesn't Want to Have Sex" was one headline, "Dating a Musician" was another.

The readers had been on their best behavior for a few weeks after my mom died, writing the kindest comments—sometimes too kind. I could tell they were scared to upset me. But soon enough, they were back to behaving like a real family, mocking each other, giving tough love to the letter writer, and, when necessary, telling me I had it all wrong. I liked it when it was normal again, even with the occasional trolls.

The thing that surprised me the most after my mother's death was how much everyone else continued to live. Jess's husband got a job in Florida, so her version of happily-ever-after moved to a new state. I got a better credit card for miles so I could see her as much as possible.

Brette and Ben grew closer. Mark's kids got taller and started to make weird and questionable jokes, just like their dad.

The couple that met through the *Love Letters* comments section decided to get married. Coincidentally, they scheduled the wedding for my birthday.

Another person ready for new experiences was Patrick. He'd started dating a woman he'd met through his sister-in-law, and he looked sheepish when I asked if it was serious. His expression told me he hoped it was. I was rooting for him.

♡

Not long before my mom died, maybe months before those last days in the hospital, she started crying—that manic half-happy, half-miserable cry brought on by exhaustion and chemo and too many feelings at once. She told me, during that session of weepiness, that she was afraid she had done it all wrong.

"I didn't spend enough time on friends," she said. "I was too determined to get married again. I was too focused on romance."

She'd noticed that it was our friends, as opposed to the great romantic loves, who kept us entertained, gave us hope, and made us feel safe when life was at its scariest. Even *Love Letters* had taught her that, she said. The more connections, the more comments, the better.

"You have a beautiful life," my mom said. "It's because

you weren't focused on getting married or always having a boyfriend. You did it right."

"I'm not so sure," I told her. "I don't think we're supposed to forgo love and romance for friendship. I think we're all supposed to do all of it—to try to have romantic love and close friends, and everything in between."

"It's not easy to find both," my mom said. "It's so easy to get lost in one and miss out on the other."

"Right," I agreed. "So we just have to do our best and stay surrounded by good people."

She would have been pleased by how that idea was represented at her funeral.

The event, which was more of a recital, was held in a local bed-and-breakfast. A few of her longtime piano students traveled to Boston to perform.

Their audience included familiar faces from Maryland, *Boston Globe* staffers, Brette's friends from New York, and some men we'd loved. I remember that Harry was there, without his younger brother. Patrick stood in the back of the room guarding the door like a bouncer.

My mom's oncologist was there. My dad was not. I was told that Draco had wanted to attend, but that one of our mutual friends advised him not to come. I wouldn't have minded.

♡

Since she's been gone, I stay surrounded as often as possible. I keep my friends close and try to be good to them. I attempt to show them how grateful I am that they continue to stick around.

I take the train to New York City a lot so I can watch television with Brette while Ben blows glass up the street.

I fly to Florida and watch Jess's boys become little men. They call me "Meremith."

I watch the Rachels approach their thirties with trepidation and some relief. They are figuring out how to make themselves so happy that they forget to post it all on social media. They are learning when to use the shrug emoji instead of all of those knives and toilets.

Sometimes that Yo-Yo Ma album I downloaded in the hospital comes up in my gym mix, and I find myself on the elliptical machine with my eyes closed as the cello booms through my earbuds. Sometimes I hear "Brand New Day," a Sting song my mom loved but I always felt was cheesy, and I turn it all the way up. I try to be less cynical and to think of it as an anthem.

I visit the vampires, but I don't let them take too much of my time. I remind myself that they aren't going anywhere. They are immortal, after all.

I date. It can be scary and annoying, but sometimes I get a blowout and wear a dress with a waistline, and allow myself to imagine the possibilities.

When I get overwhelmed or lonely, I think of the letter writers who feel the same, and I attempt to take my own advice.

I do my best to connect with other people, to be a better listener, because I'm pretty sure that's the point.

But I don't know for certain.

I don't have all the answers.

Readers: What do you think?

Epilogue

Sometimes letter writers never want to hear from me again. Other times, they keep in touch and send me updates.

There's no such thing as closure, but there are continuations. Developments.

Here's how some of the problems played out after they were written.

THE UPDATES

SHOULD I GIVE UP ON MARRIAGE?

PAGE 191

"Dave" and I are still very happily together…not married. After this letter was published, I took a long, hard look at myself and thought, "Why do I want this so badly?" I realized that the environment around us was pressuring us more than anything, and I thought that since everyone else was doing it, we should, too. I thought, "I will lose him if I don't marry him!" And that was not a great way of thinking.

What I learned from your column, therapy, and other letters I have read is that everyone has a different timeline when it comes to love. Right now—and what I have had for the past six years—is someone who is committed, loving, and providing. He is a better partner than most husbands I have met. His main block was finances, and, more recently, he was laid off, so we are back to trying to save up for a house and future again.

One thing we can agree on is that we have a future together, and that's all that matters to me. I don't need to be his wife for people to take us seriously. He is my family, and a ring on my finger or a certificate isn't going to change a thing. Like I said, if it happens, that's great and we will celebrate it our way, but I'm okay with it not happening or waiting, because in the end, I got what I wanted: the partner who is perfect for me.

SEX AFTER CANCER

PAGE 181

A few years ago, we did go to therapy for about three months and it just didn't work. We still live in the same house but live two different lives.

He doesn't help with the kids at all. He will come to a few of their activities if it is convenient for him. He doesn't help around the house. We don't plan anything together. We don't share a bedroom. He is basically living as a tenant in my home.

I am concerned about how this will affect my kids' view of marriage. I have thought about having him move out; I have a good job and could easily support myself. It would probably make me feel better about myself. I have great friends and family, the best kids in the whole world, and a very good job. I'm happy in all aspects of my life except my marriage.

IS ONLINE DATING REQUIRED?

PAGE 145

I'm still single, I still hate online dating, I still don't have a better idea to meet someone. I did join a couple of MeetUp groups and get a lot of emails, but have completely failed to follow through on actually going to things (which, I understand, is the crucial part of the process). I should work on that. Some commenters did hit the nail on the head: I am wishing for the impossible scenario of skipping dating to head right to a relationship. I don't like being called lazy, but they may have a point.

Others correctly surmised that there was something else going on...namely a colleague/friend-with-benefits situation that predictably went awry. That hasn't been Love Letter #2 because I know the answer to that one: stop being a dumbass and move on. It's hard to start over with someone new when there's someone I think I'd be great with five feet away...all the time...including right now. There's a lot more to that story, but I know what I have to do.

DATING WITH A CHRONIC ILLNESS

PAGE 109

When I wrote to Love Letters years ago, I was very sick and battling bouts of serious depression (although I did not want to acknowledge it at the time). After lots of research and finding the right doctor, I discovered that my chronic pain was caused by trigeminal neuralgia (irritated/damaged cranial nerves) and I am happy to report that I am pain-free. To be able to write that last sentence makes the last two years seem like a dream.

Not long after my diagnosis, I met a wonderful man. He is truly kind and generous—a real "genuine article" as my great-grandmother would say. He has some health challenges of his own, which he bravely shared when we first started dating. In a way, my own experiences continue to help me to be a compassionate and supportive partner—because I can empathize with his feelings of uncertainty and frustration regarding his health. Whatever challenges lie ahead, I am confident that we can face them together.

Thank you all for your advice all those years ago. Many comments helped me to step outside of the narrative I had built in my own head and consider different points of view. Most of all, your comments lifted me up at a time when I needed it most. LL readers, never stop being amazing!

OUR FIFTEEN-YEAR AGE GAP

PAGE 97

I sent that letter in a weak moment and while I do not regret it, I was both amused and kind of surprised at many of the responses, particularly that I was living off divorce money (laughable—I work very hard) or that I was trying to brag about my life and situation (absolutely not the case).

My relationship is very strong and we recently purchased a house (together) and while neither of us wants to get married, we have a pretty happy life. It's definitely not perfect and we certainly have our issues. They are never age-related and are pretty typical relationship problems. I have come to a point in our relationship where I truly do not think about our age difference and care little about what others think.

SHE WANTS TO PROPOSE TO HER BOYFRIEND

PAGE 193

I wish I had a happier update. My then-boyfriend is now my future ex-husband. We are currently going through a contentious divorce. It is eye-opening to read this letter, especially the part: "He would like to have all the money saved up before he proposes." We ended up basically eloping, rushing into marriage without discussing personal finances, philosophy on managing money, or expectations on how we would do so. We did talk about marriage and having a family a lot—in a clearly romanticized fashion. Our marriage has almost financially ruined me, and I was surprised to learn that he had absolutely no savings, owed back taxes, and the list goes on and on in terms of his personal financial mess.

I am of the mind-set that money is just money, and I tried to make things work financially for us and spent my entire savings to "help" our marriage, but it quickly turned into a very unequal relationship in this regard. He took advantage.

We had a beautiful and amazing child (the one thing I am grateful for from this relationship), but I was solely responsible for all of our child's expenses (and care!). To top all of this off, the divorce is costing me more than the "wedding," but I am looking forward to a day when I am legally divorced and can start a new life with my daughter; hopefully soon.

My piece of advice to the LL Community is to take the time

to really know their significant others and their financial standing and history, do not be afraid to ask questions, and expect an open and honest discussion—because maybe they are not really saving money for a ring or wedding.

SHE HOOKED UP WITH A COWORKER

PAGE 65

I marinated in the situation for a number of months before I decided that many of the commenters were right and that I could not stay in a work environment that was causing me confusion, embarrassment, and discomfort. I went on a number of interviews and ended up leaving my position there (where said coworker remains to this day). I also started dating again, toggling between two apps, and met a man I am now speeding toward marrying.

I would not go so far as to say that this (overall wonderful) relationship does not also have challenges but I love how this person treats me and how I feel when we spend time together. What else? I got a puppy. We bought a house.

I hate tautophrases, so I will not offer an "it is what it is," or even a non-tautophrase like "everything happens for a reason" to try to dismiss the events that sent me tumbling toward writing to *Love Letters*.

What I will say is that that whole span of time and the intensity of the feelings feels incredibly remote now.

I can also say with firm confidence that not a moment of my upcoming wedding day and honeymoon to follow will be colored by the person I wrote to you about. I am, however, moving forward with a much clearer sense, thanks to my husband-to-be, of what romantic relationship respect, transparency, kindness, and honesty look like.

HER SEX DRIVE OUTPACES HIS

PAGE 217

We were able to compromise by talking more about what we like and trying out new things (and times) as you suggested, so that we were both happier with our sex life! And honestly, as time went on, and I got super busy with a new job and a lot of other things going on in my life, frequency became less important to me than quality.

We actually got engaged a few months after my letter, and we are now married and expecting a baby girl in August. Being pregnant has definitely lowered my sex drive, and now I really appreciate that sex is not always the only thing on my husband's mind. Like all aspects of a relationship, I think that our sex life will always have some ups and downs, but since the "downs" are few and far between and the "ups" are much more constant, I feel very lucky and happy with our life together!

STILL HAVE FEELINGS FOR AN EX AND CO-PARENT

PAGE 164

I can't believe so many years have passed since my letter. The advice was very helpful. However, I think for unrequited love, time was the overall solution to things. I guess that saying, "Time passes. Memories fade. Feelings change. People leave. But hearts never forget" is all very true, in most every case.

WHEN DOES IT GET BETTER?

PAGE 46

The truth is, it did get better. It took a long time, but it did. It was funny—not long after I wrote in, I met a guy.

He was handsome and fun, he was the life of the party, and I no longer felt alone. We had some really great ups and some really low lows. It was exhausting, but I so badly wanted to find that love again. I remember saying to myself that nothing would ever feel like that first love; sparks like that were only reserved for that first young and innocent time.

Long story short, it took me years to realize that this relationship wasn't good for me long-term. I was trying too hard to make things work. Maybe it was because I so badly wanted to move on from that first relationship, maybe I just wanted to stop striking out. Whatever the reason, I finally realized I needed more.

I can now say that six months removed from that *second* breakup, I have found someone who makes me feel those sparks like my college ex. It's funny—you said that relationships always hit you differently, that sometimes they hit you harder than you thought they would and sometimes they barely faze you. It took me three-plus years and drastic life changes to get over my college ex (who I only dated for a year and a half), while it took me only a few months to move on from a much-longer relationship with a live-in boyfriend. I think I needed to go through both those relationships to really appreciate the one that I have now. I have that magic and shine of the first, but the pragmatism, respect, and knowledge of how to build a life with someone that came from the second.

I am so grateful for your answer to my letter and the support I felt from your followers. It took a while, but things got better.

So much better.

Acknowledgments

This book would not exist without Linda Henry, whose ideas make things better. Linda: *The Boston Globe* is lucky to have your heart and brain. This book would also not exist without the world's best boss and life strategist, Janice Page. Thank-yous also go to: John Henry; all of my excellent colleagues at the *Globe* (especially the Living/Arts department); my editor at Grand Central, Suzanne O'Neill, who saw value in this story and made me laugh while I wrote it; the marketing team at the *Globe*; Lane Zachary and Todd Shuster, who helped make this book a book; my publishing life partner and agent, Katherine Flynn; *Globe* editor Brian McGrory, who is so supportive that he let me write a book under the company name with a chapter about vampire porn; *Washington Post*/former *Boston Globe* editor Marty Baron, who is so cool he was played in a movie by an actor who has also played a sexy gangster; Joe Sullivan, Julian Benbow, Chris Gasper, Dan Shaughnessy, and the *Boston Globe* Sports Department; Trenni Kusnierek for incredible friendship (and for introducing me to Michele Steele); Lauren Iacono and Allie Chisholm, my real-life Gilmore Girls; Pete Thamel, for being there for every breakup; Benielle Sims, who runs the world (or should) and Jenny Johnson, my F.S.; Ryan Breslin; Marcia Dick, Ellen Clegg, Andrea Estes, Paula Bouknight, Kerry Drohan, and Jen Peter, who raised me; David Beard, who said "let's just put it online"; Tito Bottitta and Nicole Cammorata; Steve Greenlee; Wanda Joseph-Rollins and all librarians; Elaine Ryan, Tish Bento, and Scott Steeves, who surrounded me like a never-ending plant; Charlotte Vena; Aileen Gallagher and Syracuse friends; Mark Morrow; Thomasine Berg; June Wulff; Katie Locke for skills and enthusiasm; my men: Santo, Alex, and Gabe Perez; Sarah Grafman; Ed Ryan for teaching me the rules of the road; Tina Valinsky and Shirley Craig; Nancy, Tim, Ariela, Elana, and Sarah Knight; the Goldstein Cleveland Bureau (Brad, Julie, Yael, Sam, Nate, Shula, and Jacob); Sacha Pfeiffer (and Hansi); David Dahl; Joanna Odorisio, who read early drafts of this book and *Game of Thrones* at the same time; Cassidy DeStefano who kept me on track; Emily Mitchell who made sure I finished; Devin Smith for all things social; Liz Arcury for jokes; Wesley Morris and his mom for love I will never forget; the international Susanna Fogel; my Skyscraper, Sara Faith Alterman; Greg Klee; Yvonne Abraham; Beth Teitell; Scott Helman; Sadaf Ahsan; Lauren Shea and Heather Ciras for many texts; Rachel Zarrell for being my first—and a force; Linda Reisman; Desaray Smith for twenty-five years of friendship and a red pen; the incredible Francie Latour; Chris Mayer; Hayley Kaufman and Rachel and Nate and Devin; Cheryl Holland; Carly Sitrin; filmmaker Heather MacDonald; Ty Burr, in general; my new Factory partner, Joani

Geltman; Christine Yoon and Matt Ellis; Bryan Barbieri, my treat; Teresa Hanafin and Steve Morgan for so much time and thoughtfulness; David Goldstein, who attempts comebacks; Rachel Raczka for giving me all of the love, sometimes with Pepper on it; Paul, Ralphie, Emily, Paul Sr., and Kate Faircloth for board games and a home; the Faircloth-affiliated Margaret Willison; Michael Fitzgerald; Rebecca Ostriker; Paul Makishima; the Piggot crew, a.k.a. Matthew Gilbert, Joan Anderman, Katie Johnston, James Reed, Christopher Muther, Devra First, Tim Flynn, and team leader Sarah Rodman, with whom I'd go anywhere; the brilliant and encouraging Mark Feeney; Sophie Charles and Fran Forman for being my family (and for sharing Bob, Josh, Hannah, and Rocco); Paul Bernon, for trust and hang time; Ann and Jim Lano; Gina Favata and Jon Gorey; Casey Ross and Beth Healey; Brenda Pollock; Kathy Levine for coming to Maryland; the great Emily Procknal; the companionship and laundry machines of Nicole Lamy and Michael Patti (and Cal, Malcolm, and June!); Paul Colton, Jim Matte, Bill Herzog, Rich Kassirer, and the copy editors I never take for granted; Chris Chinlund and Dan Wasserman; the Barocas family; Ben Barocas, who is beloved by so many Goldsteins; Jason Notte, who pried that Timberwolves T-shirt out of my hands; Michelle McGonagle and Julia and Beckett Shanahan, who welcomed me like Weasleys; Brad White for calmness; Mark Shanahan, forever first under my favorites; Margo Howard, for the best advice; Jenn Abelson, Danielle Kost, and Jessica Douglas-Perez, whom I hug every second of the day (in my mind); Brette Goldstein for making me happy and supporting me for literally my whole life; and my mom, Leslie Goldstein, and all of the music she left behind.

The most important thank you goes to the people who read and interact with Love Letters—especially those mentioned in this book. I won't reveal your names, but you've saved me more times than you know. I wake up grateful for you every day, and, after nine years, I'm still totally into you.

About the Author

Meredith Goldstein is an advice columnist and entertainment reporter for *The Boston Globe.* She began writing *Love Letters*, her daily dispatch of wisdom for the lovelorn, in 2009. The column inspired her memoir/essay collection, *Can't Help Myself.* Meredith is also the author of the young adult novel *Chemistry Lessons* (2018), which follows a teen scientist who uses research to fix a breakup, and *The Singles* (2012), a novel about a group of dateless guests at a wedding. Meredith was born in New Jersey, raised in Maryland, and lives in Boston with a David Bowie doll and a full-size cotton candy machine. Visit Meredith at MeredithGoldstein.com